SWAMI DAYANAND AND THE 1857 REVOLUTION

SWAMI DAYANAND AND THE 1857 REVOLUTION

A K GANDHI

LAUNCHPAD

An imprint of
Srishti Publishers & Distributors

Srishti Publishers & Distributors
A unit of AJR Publishing LLP
212A, Peacock Lane
Shahpur Jat, New Delhi – 110 049
editorial@srishtipublishers.com

First Published by Launchpad,
An imprint of Srishti Publishers & Distributors in 2026

10 9 8 7 6 5 4 3 2 1

This is a work of non-fiction based on the author's research. Some events have been fictionalised for dramatic effect. While due care has been taken to verify all information at press time, any inadvertent miss brought to notice shall be updated in the subsequent editions. The views expressed in the book are the author's own and are not intended to hurt the sentiments of any individual, community, sect, group, or religion.

Foreword

Being aligned with Dharma is not merely one's own spiritual progress through silent *tapasya* or meditation. Rather, its ultimate objective is to find its fullest expression for selfless service to the society's well-being. Tapasya is not mere meditation and religious work, but it can very well be a period of silent national service, which brings about change in the society without expecting public recognition or reward. This doctrine is in consonance with the basic tenets of the Hinduism, in which spirituality and patriotism are interwoven concepts. The two together bring peace and progress.

While we may be aware of the significance of Swami Dayanand's public teachings and literature, yet what is equally significant is the silent and unknown period during which he persevered in quiet effort and sacrifice for over three years. This period of silent tapasya has remained unseen, unknown and beyond public scrutiny for numerous decades. It is this unknown period which has led to wild conjectures, leading to divergent views among historians as well as the followers of the Arya Samaj.

The author is not a follower of the Arya Samaj, yet his curiosity deserves appreciation for he chose a subject that is both subtle and demanding, as it pertained to the undocumented period of Maharshi Dayanand's life. This work requires patience, balance and intellectual honesty, which he has displayed in abundance. His effort has been proven worthy by the fact that he has been able to bring out the truth behind this unknown period. He has devoted himself in long, intensive research and field work. As he worked, he realised that the more he dived, the more spectacular the revelations were. The pieces of evidence were scattered over so wide an expanse that it took him almost six years to collect, collate and cross-refer them. During the process, he solemnly worked to analyse the clues that appeared relevant and were founded in some evidence. The outcome of this prolonged process has been spectacular and mindboggling. His meticulous hard work has resulted into a viable treatise that can fascinate anyone who is interested in hidden pearls of history.

The outcome of this tapasya was the occurrence of the 1857 Uprising that has proved an important milestone in the country's history. His insight behind his contribution in this Uprising is proven by the fact that it shook the very foundations of the East India Company's rule. Not only this, it also instilled an awakening among people to realise the importance of freedom and standing against atrocities by the foreign masters, and to inspire them to achieve what was legitimately theirs. We have a great lesson to draw from this study of the unknown period – True patriotism often works in silence. It works to achieve its objective through righteousness, reform, education and social awakening to oppose injustice, suppression and atrocity.

This book links the scattered pieces of evidence, by which the realization dawns that during this phase of purposeful anonymity, Swamiji was putting his life at stake for national service without an expectation of recognition or reward. During this effort, he answered to the call for courage, restraint, moral clarity and readiness for sacrifice. It becomes evident that his ultimate goal of elevating himself to spiritual height blended well with the uplift of all his countrymen. He has brilliantly exhibited through his unknown period how *tapasya, sadhana* and *dhyan* can very well be the pillars of active, dignified social and national life. The Arya

Samaj, founded by him, has continued to uphold his ethos even today.

However, there remains a division of opinion among certain sections regarding whether Swami Dayanand Saraswati played a role in instigating the Great Revolt of 1857. This work, through its specific and credible evidence, possesses the ability to decisively address and resolve this long-standing divide.

Furthermore, the Hindi feature film '1857 Diary – the Hidden Pages', whose credits also include the name of the author, powerfully brings to light the real and hitherto concealed contribution of Maharshi Dayanand Saraswati to the Great Revolution of 1857. Inspired by the ideals of Swarajya and Swadharma, the film will undoubtedly acquaint audiences with the hidden truths and untold dimensions of the revolution.

It was my pleasure to have met the author on two occasions - one at Tankara, the birthplace of Maharishi, and the other at Meerut. It was at the latter place that I got an opportunity to watch him present the facts and arguments before the audience; and this adequately convinced me that his research work matches the highest standards of field work, scholarly wisdom, and historical insight. This book reaches the exalted heights of unravelling a mystery that has baffled the world for such a long period of time. Through his sincere effort, he has brought out several unknown pearls of evidence which go on to convince what Maharishi was busy doing during the unknown period. In this effort, he has worked long and hard, and the time has come to acknowledge the authenticity of his endeavour. He has displayed his acumen through a number of works he has penned so far, and this work is a true masterpiece, the feather of his cap and his magnum opus in true sense of the word.

It is a matter of great elation that this research work settles the public opinion about Maharishi's contribution in the great Revolution of 1857. I am hopeful that this book will also inspire the youth to understand that true patriotism and true spirituality are like two sides of the same coin.

With blessings,
–Swami Sachchidanand

Reverential Gratitude

A large number of people have rendered their invaluable assistance in the writing of this historical work. They include historians, scholars, religious scholars, and common people. It was not possible to meet some of them in person owing to various reasons, but a fruitful discussion took place with them all via one or the other medium. We are humbled by their knowledge and learning, without which it would not have been possible to have written this book at this level. We would like to name the following personalities for their role and aid specifically:

- Dr. Sushil Kumar Bhati, Historian
- Dr. K.K. Sharma, Historian
- Dr. K.D. Sharma, Historian
- Dr. Kiran Singh, Historian
- Dr. Amit Pathak, Historian
- Prof. Vighnesh Kumar, Historian
- Mr. Prabhakar, Scholar, Ajmer
- Mr. Rajendra Jigyasu, Scholar and Author, Abohar
- Acharya Sanjay Dev, Scholar, Ajmer
- Dr. Gaur, Scholar, Ajmer
- Er. Adityamuni Vanasprasth, Author, Bhopal
- Dr. Akhilesh Chandra Sharma, Scholar, Indore
- Mr. Rampal Singh, Principal, Sikri High School, Village Sikri Khurd
- Mr. Harbir Singh, Village Sikri Khurd, Meerut
- Dr. Manoj Kumar Gautam, Government Museum Meerut
- Mr. Dharmpal Singh, Former Pradhan, Village Panchli Khurd, Meerut
- Master Sattar Ahmad, Vill. Basod, Baghpat
- Mr. Shivkumar Chaprana, descendent of Dhansingh Kotwal, Vill. Panchli Khurd, Meerut
- Ch. Yashpal Singh, Descendent of Shahmal, Vill Bijrol, Baghpat

- Mr. Dharmveer, Vill. Gagol, Meerut
- Mr. Harveer Singh Taliyan, Pradhan, Arya Samaj Sabha, Meerut
- Mr. Shivkumar Sharma, Descendent of Acharya Deepankar, Meerut
- Mr. Mahavir Singh, Principal (Retd), Government Inter College, Meerut
- Aryamuni Vanaprastha (Laxmichandra Arya), Translator, Author and Scholar, Meerut
- Lt. Col. Amardeep Tyagi, Meerut
- Mr. Vedpal Shastri, Freedom Fighter and Principal (Retd), Dayanand College, Gurukul Inter College, Vill. Dorli, Meerut
- Vimla Bahinji, Vyas Ashram, Haridwar
- Shanti Bahinji, Thinker, Vyas Ashram, Haridwar
- Dr. R.K. Bhatnagar, IAS, Convener, INTACH, Meerut

Chapter

We are thankful to Prashant Agarwal for his help in sketching the route march taken by the sepoys.

We are also thankful to the following organisations for their kind contribution:

- Paropakarini Sabha, Ajmer
- INTACH (Indian National Trust for Art and Cultural Heritage), New Delhi & Meerut
- Vyas Ashram, Haridwar
- Arya Samaj Sabha, Meerut
- Bharatiya Prajnan Parishad, Meerut

I should pay my gratitude to my wife and eternal source of inspiration, Alka Gandhi for her long company on my research trips across states. My children—Mohit, Aneesha and Sanchit also deserve acknowledgement for providing their perspective on several points. I should also take this opportunity to thank Suhail Mathur of The Book Bakers for his excellent services as a literary agent. In the end, I would also like to thank Srishti Publishers for publishing the English edition of this research work. In this connection, I should appreciate the efforts of Arup Bose, the Publisher, and team Srishti for their insightful contribution towards bringing this work into reality.

Preface

The 1857 Uprising was neither the first nor the last of its kind in India. Most other revolutions remained centred and limited to a specific area with only one segment of people taking part, while others remained mute spectators; for instance, only the sepoys took part in the 1806 Vellore Uprising, only landlords participated in the 1804-17 uprising in Odisha, and only tribals took part in the Santhal revolt. So it was not the case with this one. It was a complete revolution in the sense that Hindus and Muslims, civilians and sepoys, landlords and rulers, farmers and tribals, villagers and city-dwellers took an active part together. This fact makes it the First War of Freedom.

The 1857 Uprising is one of the world's prominent revolutions; however, what makes it remarkable is that no single leader emerged as the unanimous leader of the insurrection that engulfed a vast area of India and continued for about 2 years. Of course, several leaders emerged at the regional level, as Rani Lakshmi Bai, Begum Hazrat Mahal, Nana Saheb Peshwa, Tatya Tope, Veer Kunwar Singh and others; similarly, several leaders emerged at the local level, as Dhansingh Kotwal, Narpat Singh, Nain Singh, Rao Kadam Singh, Shahmal and many others in the Meerut region.

What makes this spectacular outbreak is the belief that no one set it in motion. Interestingly, the name of the person who started it has remained unknown until now. Official sources and history books have referred to a Hindu Faqir, but they too remain silent about his contribution. The pertinent question for me was: Who can be given credit for sparking this great revolution? Who was this hero who set out to demolish the Company Raj and turn over a new leaf in Indian history? Who was this committed Yogi who has himself remained anonymous to the world, yet has helped etch in our memory the names of stalwarts like Mangal Pande, Lakshmi Bai, Kunwar Singh, Bakht Khan, Ahmadulla Shah, and others?

The author has made a solemn endeavour to bring out the contribution of this great man, through prolonged, earnest research, and this has taken shape in the form of the present book, which is permeated with adequate direct and circumstantial evidence as well as quotations from scholars, as well as the protagonist himself. The most breathtaking fact is that this personality is quite well-known to us, and a large number of people follow the principles he has laid down. If he has carefully kept his contribution in the 1857 Uprising concealed from public view, it was under a scheme, and this book tries to look into it too. You have seen that we have called the protagonist Sanyasi until we have sufficiently proven that it was none other than Mahrishi Dayanand Saraswati.

A salient feature of the book is that it answers all possible queries a curious reader might have about our protagonist or the 1857 Uprising. We have referred to original texts to arrive at our inferences, because several writers and so-called scholars have tried to put words in the great seer's mouth and have amended his texts or articles either out of extreme veneration or in a bid to show their articulation skills; and this has caused more harm than good. When the protagonist himself does not feel any regret in admitting his shortcomings, like taking *bhang* or narcotic leaf, or finding it hard to grasp several texts, there should be no reason for his followers to attempt to conceal them. No person can indeed be perfect.

The author, as a historian, has been working to unravel the mysteries engulfing Indian history. His work on different aspects of this massive Uprising has been monumental in the form of books like *1857 Kranti Va Krantidhara* and *Dance to Freedom*, published respectively by the National Book Trust, India, and Fingerprint Pub. I earnestly hope that this book, like my other books, will receive the grace and support of the scholarly readers as ever.

Thank you.

A.K. Gandhi
Meerut

1: March to Destiny

The year was 1855. A tall and sturdy Sanyasi was marching on foot from Ahmedabad to Haridwar, a distance well over 1000 kilometres. He was marching with an intense wish in his heart. Little did he know that he would meet his destiny before his wish could be fulfilled. Having embraced the exalted tradition of Sanyas, or renunciation of worldly life and material attachments, a Sanyasi or hermit now, he was marching alone, with a few books tied in a cotton sheet hanging from his left shoulder, a *kamandal* or an ewer in his right hand, and a thick staff in his left hand.

We will soon reveal his true identity, but we are inclined to present evidence confirming it before then. Until then, we will call him Sanyasi. This is simply because not many people believe that he accomplished the monumental feat. However, the evidence we have gathered after an equally monumental research effort would go on to affirm that it was he, and no one else, who did this.

It was no maiden march for him; he had been doing this from one place to another for almost nine years since he had abandoned his parental home, but his ardent wish had remained unfulfilled. He was hopeful that his wish would be fulfilled, fully unaware of what destiny had in store for him.

The Sanyasi was now in Haridwar, where the massive Kumbh Mela was in full swing. The largest gathering of humanity that takes place every twelve years. Most people had driven bullock carts from long distances to be part of the sacred ceremony. Wherever he looked, whichever direction he glanced, he found a sea of humanity all around. As he was there with a purpose, he did not want to be part of the crowded landscape, so he took shelter in a cave on the solitary Chandi Devi Hill, located near the eastern bank of the Ganga.

Early next day, when the sun had not risen yet, the Sanyasi had finished his morning chores, including a dip in the holy river, yoga practice and meditation, and was already walking the huge grounds on the Ganga bank where a large tent city had come up. Soon, he entered the area earmarked for the Akharas, or the tentage of different monastic orders of Sadhus or ascetics. They traditionally attend the Kumbh Mela to be part of the spectacular feature of this ancient fair – Shahi Snan (now renamed as Amrit Snan).

The Sanyasi kept walking through the Akharas looking for what he wanted. He was sure that one of these could help him accomplish his wish. He was actively contacting the prominent sages and hermits in search of a capable Guru under whose guidance he could study. It was under this process that he reached the Akhara of Swami Purnanand. This personality has been called by different names. Dewan Bahadur Harbilas Sharda has called him Purnanand and Purnashram, while Acharya Deepankar has called him Swami Sampurnanand Saraswati. He was different from Purnanand, who had earlier initiated the Sanyasi into Sanyas or hermithood at Chanod.

It is believed that at this time, Swami Purnanand was about 108 years old, yet remained completely fit and active. He had a large number of disciples. It is also believed that his disciples were undertaking revolutionary activities in different parts of the country and were chiefly engaged in passing information and spreading disaffection.

When the Sanyasi was admitted to his cottage, built of mud and weed, he was enchanted by the glorious halo that the elderly hermit possessed. Praying in his heart that his burning wish would be realised there, he bowed low. Blessing the newcomer, Swami Purnanand asked what brought him there.

"I wish to study grammar and discover wisdom."

Purnanand's face brightened up as he gazed at the promising Sanyasi's glowing face. In a soft but convincing tone, he said, "The time demands that we first discover freedom. A youth like you ought to work for the country first."

The Sanyasi, on the other hand, wanted to engage himself in nothing but study. Purnanand abruptly ended the brief meeting, saying he was much older and unable to teach him. When the Sanyasi insisted, he only said that he should better contact Swami Virajanand at Mathura. As the Sanyasi stood up to leave, he did not know why he had an inkling that his wish could be fulfilled with this sage and no one else.

A unique feature of Hinduism is that religion and patriotism are intricately intertwined; they are not considered separate. However, the youthful Sanyasi was doing just the opposite and would continue to do so for a little longer.

Dismayed, the Sanyasi walked out of the Akhara, unable to understand how he could accomplish his wish. He had seen several young disciples studying in the temporary campus. If he could teach so many of them, why could he not be one of them? This question perturbed him time and again. He then enquired about Swami Virajanand. He felt gloomy when he came to know that he was 81 years of age and had lost his eyesight in childhood. He failed to understand how a sightless person could teach him the intricate system of Sanskrit grammar.

The Sanyasi had abandoned his father's place nine years ago. He had embraced a monastic order, but his search for a Guru was yet incomplete and inconclusive. He was marching from one place to another in search of a Guru – an able teacher who could teach him Panini's *Ashtadhyayi*, a book on Sanskrit grammar, which would help him study the *Vedas* and gain wisdom that he intended to transmit to the ignorant, bonded masses under the foreign yoke. Ever since he had left home, he came in close contact with a large number of saints, hermits and holy men. However, none could quench his thirst for supreme knowledge, nor could they teach him grammar, which would help him bring out the most intimate mysteries scattered in the Vedas. Satisfied with none, he continued with his wanderings, and this was what had brought him to Haridwar.

It could not be said that his wanderings until then had been entirely fruitless. He had gathered pearls of wisdom, including the most intricate Yoga techniques, from one or the other holy man at Ahmedabad and Mount Abu, the places where he stayed for six years. All this had broadened his perspective about what he was looking for and what was of little use to him. In this process, he had discarded several schools of thought that did not convince him, yet he had miserably failed to pinpoint the doctrine that could pacify him, satisfy him, and hold up to his logic. When he came to know of the Kumbh Fair being held at Haridwar, his feet took that direction of their own accord. It was to be a remarkable confluence of the learned, the scholars, the saints and the hermits. He hoped that his objective would be fulfilled there. In his lecture on August 4, 1875, at Pune, the Sanyasi himself said:

"From there [Ahmedabad] I walked on to Haridwar. The Kumbh Fair was then in full swing."

The Kumbh Fair, held in the first half of 1855, was massive as usual. About this time, the East India Company's rule was about to complete a century. The saints and faqirs who visited from place to place led people to believe that the atrocious Company Raj would crumble at the end of one hundred years. Maybe there was no concrete plan to drive out the English, yet the people had begun to feel excited. How could the people who believed in this idea keep themselves aloof from the sea of humanity, coming to the fore as the holy Kumbh? It provided avenues to send messages to every corner of the massive land, which would otherwise not have been easy in those days. This was why it had become a lair of revolutionaries who wanted the English rule to end.

The Sanyasi, too, was aware of the underlying sentiments prevailing among the masses. However, he was not inclined to take part in any such movement. He was firm that he wished to seek only a Guru who would help him with his studies.

A look at the political spectrum in 1855 can also help us understand the unfolding events. In 1848, Lord Dalhousie, the Governor General, framed a new policy called the 'Doctrine of Lapse', a simple trick to assimilate the native princely states into the English empire. Under it, if a ruler died without a natural heir, his adopted son was not considered a legal heir, and the state was brought under the Company's direct control. This doctrine was applied to several princely states, including those of Satara, Jaitpur-Sambhalpur, Baghat, Udaipur, Jhansi, Nagpur and Karauli. Besides, if the greedy English masters accused a native ruler of incompetence, his state too was merged into the empire, as happened to Awadh in 1856. This policy caused disaffection among the native rulers, as their traditional right to adopt a child had been curbed. They viewed the policy as illegal and wished to act against the British Empire. However, there was not one princely state capable of standing up to the English might on its own. This meant that the entire country would have to come under a common banner. Nana Saheb Peshwa formulated a plan to undertake this task at the central level. In addition, several other plans were afoot in different parts of the country at different levels.

It would be appropriate to know more about Nana Saheb Peshwa. After the third Anglo-Maratha war in 1817-18, the East India Company crushed and occupied the Maratha empire. The Peshwa Bajirao II was pensioned off to Bithur (near Kanpur), fixing his pension at 80,000 pounds per annum, a princely sum by any means, which could help him lead a royal, luxurious life. Bajirao had no son, so he adopted two sons of a Deccani Brahmin courtier. The older one, Dhondu Pant, born in 1824, is now known as Nana Saheb Peshwa, also known as Nana Rao. He was made heir to the throne of Bajirao II. It is worth noting that Nana Saheb had, among his childhood playmates, Tatya Tope, Azimullah Khan, and Manikarnika Tambe (later Rani Lakshmi Bai of Jhansi). No wonder that all of them campaigned against the English simultaneously.

At the death of Bajirao II in 1851, the East India Company refused to recognise Nana Saheb as his heir, arguing that the Maratha empire no longer existed. He could no longer claim any post or designation, as he was not a natural heir. Nana Saheb entreated the Company to restore his designation and pension, but to no avail. He even sent Azimulla Khan, his Vakeel (secretary), to England in 1853 to file an appeal, but again without a positive outcome. Azimulla Khan finally returned to India in 1855.

The queen of Jhansi also deserves a mention. Manikarnika (or Manu) was married to Raja Gangadhar Rao of Jhansi. Between them, they had a son, who died in infancy. In the meantime, Gangadhar Rao too breathed his last, after which the queen adopted a son and named him Damodar Rao. Following his wily doctrine, Dalhousie fixed a pension of 60,000 rupees per annum for her and passed an order for her to quit Jhansi. Thus, she, too, had a major cause for estrangement toward the English. This happened in March 1854.

Until Azimulla Khan's return from England, Nana Saheb did not wish to run a campaign against the English. He desired only what he was entitled to, but the English arrogance forced him to plan a massive operation. He knew how powerful the English were, and he could not have carried out an open insurrection without arranging support and resources, so he set out to formulate a clandestine nationwide plan. He visited different places seeking support and cooperation from different entities. It was in this connection that he went to Haridwar, as he could contact saints and hermits, mostly classified into several akharas or monastic orders, who could play a vital role in spreading disaffection among people against the Company rule.

***

Our protagonist Sanyasi kept trying his luck with different Akharas, but to no avail. He consistently felt that only Swami Purnanand could fulfil his desire, so he approached his Akhara again a few days later. He did not have to wait long before he was brought into his audience.

Purnanand looked at the Sanyasi meaningfully, then said, very briefly, "Sit down there and see what is going to unfold here."

The Sanyasi sat down in a corner. He was confounded; all this seemed like a mystery to him. His mind endeavoured to solve it, but could arrive at no inference. Did the Swami want time to avoid him? Or was there something important going to happen? When he could decide on nothing, he just closed his eyes and tried to meditate, but his mind was clouded by various thoughts.

A little later, the Sanyasi felt some movement in the cottage. He opened his eyes to find two youths, about his age, bowing down before the Swami, who beckoned him to come near too. He searchingly gazed at the two handsome newcomers, who appeared proud and fearless. They were in ordinary dresses, but there was something unique in their personalities. Soon, he was told that they were Nana Saheb and Azimulla Khan. They had arrived there to seek Purnanand's support. However, when they learned that the elderly saint was already leading the masses in awakening against the English, they opened up and elaborated on their plan.

The Sanyasi understood that Swami Purnanand did not want him limited to studies; instead, impressed by his personality, he desired him to become a vital organ of the detailed plan.

Nana Saheb said, "We can be successful against the English only when the entire country rises in unison." He also said that his influence was as yet limited to Awadh and Bundelkhand, which was not enough. He was looking for a way to gain support in Delhi and around.

Purnanand assured him that this region would surely rise.

"But how?" Nana Saheb looked at him questioningly, "Who can accomplish this task?"

"He is right before you," Purnanand said.

The two pairs of eyes turned towards the Sanyasi. They assessed his personality and appeared impressed. "Have you spoken to him?" Nana Saheb said.

"No, I am part of no such plan," intervened the Sanyasi before Purnanand could say a word. "I want to study grammar and search for wisdom, and embroil myself in nothing else."

Nana Saheb shrank his forehead, rounding his eyes. Maybe he wondered if a massive campaign could be launched against the English with such uncertainty; however, Swami Purnanand's eyes reflected an assured, majestic smile.

Rajyogi Acharya Bhadrakam Varni mentions this meeting in the book 'Yogi Ka Atmacharitra' (Autobiography of the Yogi/Hermit), which he edited. However, this author does not agree with his account of how it occurred. Keeping the circumstantial evidence in view, this meeting must have taken place as we have discussed above. This has also been hinted at by Er. Adityamuni Vanaprasth and Dr Vedvrit 'Alok' in the book '*Apna Janmacharitra*' (Own Biography) edited by them, which speaks of the personal rendezvous between Nana Saheb and the Sanyasi. According to this book, the source of this meeting is the Sanyasi's lecture delivered in Calcutta, which came to light only after his death. In the author's personal interview with Aryamuni Vanaprasthi (formerly Lakshmichandra Sharma), who has edited Dewan Bahadur Harbilas Sharda's book, the interviewee described the entire Calcutta sermon as dubious and bogus. We will discuss this matter in some detail later in the book, so we can arrive at the truth.

2: The Mental Conundrum

It had been almost a year since our protagonist Sanyasi had attended the Kumbh at Haridwar. He utilised this period to visit several places. Despite Swami Purnanand's exhortation, he remained firm in his thinking quite obstinately. He was inclined to do nothing but study and gain wisdom; that was the higher purpose for him, which he intended to achieve, whatever might come. This purpose remained elusive, yet the Sanyasi was in no mood to relent.

Until April 1856, the Sanyasi kept walking from place to place, meeting people, reading treatises, singing devotional songs and studying different shades of the religion; however, so far as spiritual contentment was concerned, he was nowhere near it. Recently, he had cultivated an interest in 'Nari Chakra', a nervous system linked to spirituality. The topic was quite curious, yet several of its important points were beyond his grasp, as he found none who could solve them for him convincingly. Having wandered on the mountains in search of an able Guru, he headed from Kashipur (now in Uttarakhand) to the plains. He had suffered much in the hills when he had to bear with prolonged hunger and fatigue; still, he had failed to locate what he wanted. In his authentic biography, he says that from Haridwar, he visited these places: Rishikesh, Srinagar, Rudraprayag, Shivpuri, Guptakashi, Gaurikund, Badrinarayan, Rampur, Kashipur and Dronasagar.

Despite the troubles he faced in the hills, he did not want to accept defeat. He knew a true Guru could not be found without having gone through suffering. First, he set out towards

Nainital, and when he was almost there, he turned towards Garh Mukteshwar via Moradabad and Sambhal. All this while, he was resolving his doubts, so that he could pinpoint his actual goal.

Sitting on the sandy bank of the Ganga at Garh Mukteshwar, the Sanyasi was in deep thought about what he should do now. Flooded by the rising and falling emotions in his heart, the restless Sanyasi would look here and there, yet found no solace even in the splendid sight of the gurgling water of the holy river flowing right before him and expansive dense greenery beyond it. In indecision, he looked here and there only to find several bathers around on the bank. On his left stood the boat bridge connecting Delhi with Bareilly, with hardly any traffic. On his right, there were two groups of people cremating the dead bodies in a heap of dung cakes and fuel wood.

Several saints, including Swami Purnanand, had recommended Swami Virajanand as his teacher, yet he was unsure whether a blind teacher could lead him to enlightenment. All this while, the country was passing through a critical phase. Atrocities and exploitation at the hands of the British had reached their extreme. The Sanyasi wanted to keep himself limited to the discovery of learning and was not inclined to pay heed to what a number of saints and hermits had advised him, that philosophy and spirituality could not be attained in isolation from society. He was far from realising his goal, though the prevailing circumstances in the country had caused stimulation in his youthful veins. He had gone around different parts of the country. He possessed personal knowledge of what was going on around him, while spiritual wisdom was yet like a dim flame at the end of a long, dark tunnel. He had already felt a subtle change taking place in himself after he had met Swami Purnanand and Nana Saheb.

The Sanyasi was disturbed from his deep thought when he

heard a low commotion around him. He raised his head and saw people looking and wildly gesticulating towards the bridge, in the middle of which stood a man on the railing, maybe intending to commit suicide. He had hardly glanced at the man when a shot rang through the air, with which the man fell in the swiftly flowing Gangetic current, causing a little stormy ripple for a while. Then everything was as normal as before. Soon, they were hotly discussing what could have happened. When they spotted a small military squad marching out of the bridge led by a jeep, possibly occupied by a British officer, they surmised that they had shot the man. Now their discussion turned towards how the British were unleashing a wave of terror on the native people.

During his extensive wanderings, the Sanyasi had witnessed and heard of heartless atrocities committed by the foreign rulers. However, it was for the first time that he had seen such a barbaric one himself. He belonged to a tax-collecting family and had experienced the plight of farmers, who were severely oppressed by unjustly high land revenue demands. He sank into deep contemplation, more undecided than ever before. He felt a transformation occurring within himself. Rising emotions fueled a nationalistic spirit that seemed unstoppable. His thoughts went round in a whirlwind—should I continue with my search or raise a battle cry against the savage imperialists? Feeling restless and agitated, he stood up and paced along the sandy bank for quite some time to regain his tranquil mindset; however, it seemed bent on revolting. Unable to find any succour, he sat down and shut his eyes, thinking that meditation would help him get quietude. To his dismay, he was unable to concentrate. He was perplexed, as he had yet to find the path to wisdom, and his mind was now drifting in a new direction altogether.

Something occurred at Garh Mukteswar that completely

transformed his mindset; we speculate this happened as we have described above, as we have only a feeble indication of it. The English found that casting the corpses into the mighty river was a convenient way to get rid of people they considered troublesome.

Feeling dejected, the protagonist Sanyasi reopened his eyes and looked to the mighty Ganga. Not far from the bank, he saw a corpse, bloated from being in the water for a long time. It was for sure not the one that had been cast some time before. Then he decided something.

For the past few days, he had found himself taking an interest in the Nari-Chakra. According to this theory, seven points in the body's nervous system emanate energy, and *Kundalini* operates on their basis. He stood up and drew the body to the bank. He took out his knife, which helped him get food in the forest. He began cutting the body at potential Nari-Chakra points, but he failed to locate any. He took out the heart and examined it. The corpse was nothing like what was described in the books. As per his biography, these books were *Sibsanda Hat-pradipika, Yoga-bij* and *Gherand Samhita*. With this, his interest in yet another doctrine had ended. He immersed the body back into the water, then cast the related books as well. The Sanyasi has narrated this incident in his biography in these words:

> "I resolutely entered the water and soon brought the dead body out and laid it on the bank. I then proceeded to cut it open with a large knife in the best manner I could. I took out and examined the Kamal [heart], and cutting the body from the navel to the ribs, and a portion of the head and neck, I carefully examined and compared them with the descriptions in the books. Finding that they did not tally at all, I tore the books to pieces and threw them into the river after the corpse. From that time, gradually I came to the

> conclusion that with the exception of the *Vedas*, *Upanishads*, *Patanjali* and *Sankhya* all other works upon science and Yoga were false."

Frustrated and uncertain, the Sanyasi bid adieu to the Ganga and walked off. He had been roaming around the length and breadth of the land, yet without a convincing clue to his ambition. He had learnt Yoga but knew that he could achieve perfection in it only under a proficient teacher. He was aware that true wisdom could not be attained without perseverance. However, being unable to find a learned Guru, he had been groping in the dark for several years now.

So far, the only name that had made a strong pitch on his psyche was that of Swami Virajanand. He was, however, undecided whether he should go and seek his company because of his blindness since childhood; he wondered how he could lead him to enlightenment.

Another teacher who could help him realise his goal was Purnanand, whom he had met at Haridwar. However, Purnanand wanted his active contribution to the freedom struggle. His wide travels had taught him that it was not so simple a task, as the English were all-powerful, both economically and militarily, and the common masses could not confront them on their own. There was no native ruler in the entire country who could unite all people to take on the foreign masters. The truth remained that they all could not be united because of their petty vested interests. A number of small-scale uprisings had occurred even before, which failed to spread. The English could be driven out only when a large portion, if not the entire land, stood up united against them. The situation was drastic, and gaining freedom from the English seemed almost impossible to him, mainly because of disunity. The only ray of hope was an uprising by the native sepoys presently serving the English masters. This too was not an easy task, as they were posted across a wide area, and contacting them all required massive resources that were not available anywhere. Moreover, inciting them was better thought than done. The British had emerged as the most important source of employment. At the same time, the sepoys had earned some social standing as their income was stable and satisfactory amidst the disappearing jobs and a worsening economy. The uprising at Vellore had occurred over religious symbols, and no such cause existed at present. Whatever causes on which the sepoys could be incited were minor and trivial. In toto, the entire situation was quite hopeless.

For once, the Sanyasi thought of heading to Meerut, which was not very far away, and joining the effort against the English. Until now, he had been determined to attain transcendental wisdom, but what he saw today at the Garh Mukteshwar bridge left him fretful, indecisive, and shaken. He tried to maintain his composure somehow and decided to stick to his original goal – to seek a Guru. He looked up to the heavens and murmured to himself that he should continue his search for a Guru in Ayodhya, Prayagraj, or Banaras, three of the most important pilgrimage centres, and, if he failed, he would go to Mathura.

He filled his kamandal with Ganga water and walked away, taking the road along the holy river; his immediate destination was Kanpur. He kept walking along the Ganga, passing through Bulandshahr, Aligarh, Kasganj, Farrukhabad, Kannauj, and Bithur, and arriving in Kanpur. Nana Saheb lived in Bithur (in Kanpur). In his autobiography, the Sanyasi has stated that when he crossed Srangirampur to enter Kanpur, taking the road east of the cantonment there, the Samvat year of 1912 was completed, that is, it was April 5, 1856. It was just two weeks before that Nawab Wajid Ali Shah, who was expelled from his princely state of Awadh by the British on fictitious grounds, had sailed through Kanpur and met Nana Saheb's officials. You will read about its evidence a few pages later. It is very likely that our protagonist, Sanyasi, got involved in this planning, as he had already met Nana Saheb at Haridwar.

No wonder that all towns and several villages between Garh Mukteshwar and Kanpur had a massive British presence and had witnessed massive insurrection during the 1857 Uprising. Bithur and Kanpur witnessed a massive insurrection under Nana Saheb, while Bulandshahr rose under Nawab Walidad Khan. He felt an undercurrent of opposition to the British at all these places that fell en route. In contrast, he could clearly feel that people were quite vocal at Bithur and Kanpur. He now felt that the land was gradually embracing itself to take on the imperialist masters. Despite this, he presumably stuck to his original goal of finding a teacher for himself.

In his autobiography, the Sanyasi further states that he visited several places between Kanpur and Allahabad during the following five months. At the beginning of Bhadrapad (September 1856), he arrived at Mirzapur and reached Banaras the following month. He met several scholars in these places, but he found none of them whom he could embrace as his teacher, so he writes explicitly that he stayed there for twelve days, "and renewed my travels after what I sought for".

The point to note here is that he had miserably failed to find a Guru in all these places, even as he perceived restlessness among the people. Whomever he talked to, the conversation spontaneously reflected anti-British sentiments building up everywhere. He could not stay in Banaras for long, as he felt a strong, underlying revolutionary current there. The Shastris he met there all told him about the injustice the British had inflicted on their innocent king, Chait Singh, when he was arrested in 1780 on fictitious grounds. In the coming days, Babu Kunwar Singh would give the British jitters in the area.

Dismayed at not finding a Guru even in Banaras, the Sanyasi decided to make one last bid at Chunar, as someone had pointed out, and if he failed there too, he would go to Mathura. At Chunar, then called Chandalgarh, he stayed for ten days. Here, too, he found the people equally volatile as they still nursed memories of the heinous crimes that Hastings had committed when he was forced to retreat from Banaras in 1780.

Wherever the Sanyasi went, he found there seemed to be no way to find a Guru without taking part in the uprising for which people seemed to be preparing. He still wanted to stick to studying grammar and the Vedas. He decided to visit Mathura, embrace Swami Virajanand as his Guru, and do his bidding, even if it meant participating in the insurrection. Of course, in his autobiography, he speaks of going to the source of the Narmada from Chunar. However, he does so only to conceal his participation in the 1857 Revolution, because revealing it could mar the very aim he had set for himself. The way the British wreaked vengeance on anyone who opposed them meant that any admission of taking part in the Uprising would most probably have nipped this ambition in the bud, which played a vital role in national life.

The Sanyasi had traversed along the Ganga on his way to Chunar; now he took the route along the Yamuna, for which he first arrived at Prayagraj. As he finally arrived at Mathura along the route adjacent to the Yamuna, we can deduce that it was no mere coincidence that most of the towns on this route, including Aligarh and Agra, too, rose massively against the British in 1857.

It would be pertinent to note that there are three biographies/ autobiographies of the Sanyasi, and we have quoted from the one accepted as authentic. It was the one published in a periodical called '*The Theosophist*' in three instalments. We will discuss all three of them in detail later in the book.

Before proceeding, I would like to ask my readers a simple question. A person who has been describing small, trivial, insignificant incidences in his biography, such as cutting open a dead body, staying in a cave, drinking milk at one place, giving up eating rice altogether, 'someone giving me a staff for safety in the forest but I threw it away', and many others of the sort; but then he forgoes discussing about three full years of his life – what can we make out of this approach? A person who has been telling about each small and large place and town he visited, and then avoids mentioning any place from about September-October 1856; we can assume he must have been doing something he did not want to talk about.

This question becomes even more relevant when we find that during these years he himself admitted having visited a number of garrison towns; and this period of three years is the one in which the great upheaval known as the 1857 Uprising, or the first war of independence, occurred.

Doubtless, this great Sanyasi had decided to keep this period under wraps. This suspicion grows stronger when we find that he ended his biography abruptly and inconclusively. He had been wandering in search of a goal, describing each occurrence he experienced and each place he visited, when he fell silent abruptly. During his ten-year wanderings, he does not describe the English anywhere. It is not possible that he never came across the East India Company government at some point, which was a predominant power in the region. It's clear he has deliberately obliterated the entire context.

His intention behind turning this period into an envelop of

mystery becomes evident because he foresaw that the Uprising was destined to fail; it was precisely what ultimately happened. Such massive campaigns could not be inflamed every few years. This was the reason he did not wish to take part in it from the very outset, but the situation forced him to do just the opposite. Evidently, he hid this period of his life, as revealing it could become a major roadblock in achieving the higher goal he had set for himself. As he foresaw, the English meted out the harshest punishment to each one who was somehow linked to the 1857 Uprising, directly or indirectly. It is a proven fact that they destroyed the entire village when only one of its residents was found involved in it. For the Sanyasi, the higher, sublime goal was to preserve people's culture, to enable the citizens to discern good from bad, and to cause their individual, spiritual and social development, which could be realised through studying the Vedas and spreading the wisdom among his countrymen. This was the sublime goal for which he had abandoned his house and family, and had been leading a life full of wanderings and difficulties. He knew only an able teacher could help him realise his goal.

After the Sanyasi grew popular with a large following, he said on more occasions than one, "Before my death, I would reveal the names of my parents and the course of previous life. If I do this now, things will go topsy-turvy." He used the Hindi word '*golmal*' (chaos) to describe this. This statement has two parts: one related to his family and the other to his wanderings and travels since he abandoned his house. He had met his father soon after leaving home, so revealing the names and details of his family members would not matter much. It is certainly the other part that he was unwilling to tell anything about. There is little that any hermit would like to conceal; it was for sure his participation in the 1857 Uprising which could attract the British wrath, leading to the very destruction of the noble goal for which he aspired to dedicate his life. We will reveal the relevant evidence throughout this book.

After this anonymous period, the same Sanyasi displays his nationalistic spirit; not only that, he directly remarks on the 1857 Uprising. We can make a solemn effort to analyse a part of this approximately three-year period, using a little imagination and the available circumstantial evidence.

To find out the truth of this Sanyasi's personality, it would be incumbent upon us to study what he wrote and spoke on different occasions. The foremost question arises: If he has kept mum about three years of his life, does it signify concealing the truth? To answer this, let us examine his definition of truth. He writes:

> "...That is, I have understood the light of true meaning by propounding as truth what is true, and as falsehood what is false. That cannot be called true when truth is presented as falsehood and falsehood is presented as truth. Truth is to write and accept a thing as it really is. A biased person is inclined to present his falsehood as truth and the opponent's truth as falsehood, so he cannot be a supporter of truth. So, the chief task of scholars is to reveal before all people the form of truth and falsehood through delivering sermons and writing articles. After this, they should realise what is good and what is bad for them and accept the truth and discard the falsehood in order to live in bliss forever."

At another place, he writes that what is favourable to the universal chronology is true, and what is opposed to it is false. However, he nowhere states that hiding a fact will fall under truth or falsehood. A relevant question arises: Can a lower truth be disguised for the attainment of a higher goal? There is a clear distinction between 'disguising' and 'lying'. He never lied anywhere; however, he disguised the fact so that he could accomplish a more sublime purpose. When he obliterates any mention of the three-year-long period of his life, this cannot be but on purpose.

His heart was now overflowing with nationalism. At the same time, he felt it was equally essential to attain the goal he had originally set for himself. Despite this, it appeared to him that freedom from English slavery was not possible, so he decided to set out in search of wisdom, erudition, and enlightenment, but he was inclined to believe that he would work for freedom in case his final goal could not be realised without it. He never knew that he had set foot on a path that would make it possible to realise both goals simultaneously. God helps him who helps himself. The Sanyasi, until now little known, was now set to attain glory, but he would have to pass through a test. He headed to Mathura just for that.

3: Wish Fulfilled but...

Our protagonist, Sanyasi, had heard about Swami Virajanand from several people, including scholars and saints. It appears that he was told about him for the first time during his visit to Haridwar two years ago. B.K. Singh, in his book published by the National Book Trust, India, writes that this occurred in 1854. Babu Debendranath Mukhopadhyay has written that the Sanyasi heard about the blind sage from Purnanand Swami, and expressed his desire to become his disciple. At this, the elderly Purnanand said he could not admit him as his disciple because of his age. He advised him to go to Mathura instead and approach Swami Virajanand. When the Sanyasi enquired about the latter, he found that he had been blind since childhood, so he was doubtful if he would make an able Guru. Having failed in his prolonged search for an able Guru, he ultimately decided to visit Swami Virajanand at least once, as many people had admired him for his qualities as a teacher.

Swami Virajanand had lost his eyesight because of smallpox when he was just five years old. He lost his parents in childhood, and owing to the harassment of other family members, he abandoned his house and left for Haridwar. He embraced Sanyas or hermithood and began studying grammar, soon gaining complete command over it. His sojourns at various places brought him into contact with several rulers, who were very impressed by his learning and wisdom. Finally, Virajanand selected Mathura as his abode, where he opened a school in a rented building and taught Vedic scriptures. The expenditure of this school was shared among three rulers: Maharaja Balwant Singh of Bharatpur, Maharaja Ram Singh of Jaipur, and Maharaja Vinay Singh of Alwar. Besides, a number of other visitors also contributed to the expenses. Gradually, the number of pupils at the school rose as he used uniquely interesting methods and techniques to help them grasp the essence. He did not charge his pupils any fee. He was probably 78-79 years old, when the Sanyasi approached him at the close of 1856.

Writing the Sanyasi's biography, Dewan Bahadur Harbilas Sharda has given a quotation from the well-known French scholar and writer Romain Rolland:

> "...met at Mathura an elderly hermit named Swami Virajanand, who had grown blind in childhood, and took him as his Guru. He had been living in the world all alone right from the age of eleven years, and was harsher than... when it came to opposing superstitions and weakness."

The blank spaces above can be understood as the name of our protagonist, Sanyasi, whose identity we will disclose shortly.

***

The two must have interacted somewhat in this way.

The Sanyasi knocked at the door. Swami Virajanand answered from inside, "Who is it?" The Sanyasi called out his name. Then he was asked, "How can I help you?"

The Sanyasi said, "I wish to embrace Swami Virajanand as my Guru."

The next question came from behind the closed door, "What have you studied until now?"

The Sanyasi said that he had studied some grammar and other texts. The door was opened to him. He entered the room, bowed down in respect and sat down.

The pupils who approached Swami Virajanand were all young, while the Sanyasi sitting before him was about 32 years old. It is no easy task to make an old horse learn new tricks. The elderly Guru was undecided for a while, and then said, "You will have to forget all that you have learnt by now." The Sanyasi conveyed his acceptance. The next command from the Guru was: "You will have to come true on the test." The Sanyasi said that he was ready for any of them.

Virajanand said, "All right, the first test for you is to cast away in the Yamuna any un-Vedic books you have. Also, erase from your memory any learning that is contrary to the Vedas."

The young Sanyasi took to his feet immediately. He picked up the bundle of his books and went to the Yamuna bank. Without a second thought, he cast away all of them in the blue waters. Soon, he was back in the company of his Guru.

Satisfied with the Sanyasi's abidance by his command, Virajanand said that the first duty of a hermit is for his nation and society. The new disciple said he was ready to carry out any command. He was now desirous of doing good to both his country and himself.

Swami Virajanand said that the English atrocity in the country had reached its worst, and there remained no other way for liberation but to drive them out. Owing to his foot journeys across many places, the Sanyasi was well aware that it was a massive task, and that a revolution could not be brought about in the country in the absence of resources. He had some knowledge of the efforts being made towards this end, having already met Nana Saheb in Haridwar and feeling an underlying current in several towns en route, but he felt that he was working more for his princely state than for a pan-India empire. He had also perceived a revolutionary undercurrent in his wanderings ever since. The elderly Guru asked the youthful Sanyasi in definitive terms to get ready and assured him about the arrangement of resources that might be required. He concluded: "Rest assured, all of your spiritual and learning needs will be fulfilled with me."

The prospect of realising two different goals simultaneously brought an expression of self-satisfaction on the young Sanyasi's face. He was able to get rid of his mental depression after quite a while. What he now needed was a plan. A detailed discussion followed this. Some plan was already afoot; it had to be implemented, for which some preparation was underway. As they were about to rise in the end, Swami Virajanand said to the Sanyasi, "Look, I cannot see; you are not only my eyes but also my hands and feet. Above all, we are hermits; for us, spirituality is the higher, nobler goal. For us, the progress of Hinduism remains the most sublime purpose, while freedom is only an immediate one. Our contribution to this campaign has to remain limited to its explosion. Whether this campaign succeeds or fails, no harm should come to our higher goal. So, it is essential that you remain unknown; you have to hide your identity, what come may. If you feel it necessary, you may go into hiding for some time after you have completed your mission."

The Sanyasi closed his eyes for a while to ponder over all that had happened since his arrival in Mathura. He was elated that he was ultimately able to find a Guru. He thought how excellent it would be if he had come to him earlier, as he had known about him for thc past couple of years. Being such a good teacher despite blindness was an extraordinary quality. He was now sure that all his curiosities would be quenched and he would be able to get the noblest wisdom. He was required to act right from the following morning.

As the Sanyasi bowed to touch the feet of the Guru, he was told, "Have a complete rest tonight, early on the morrow we have to be on our mission."

The Sanyasi did not know where they had to go and why they had to go, but his confidence in the Guru had taken root. 'I need to go where the Guru leads me,' he murmured to himself, before he paid his respects and walked out. He was yet to make arrangements for the night's rest.

4: The Forest Meeting

In the wee hours of the following day, the sun had not yet started to redden the eastern sky when the Sanyasi, already finished with the morning chores, was now taking a dip in the cold waters of the Yamuna. It was the month of November in 1856, so the weather was already quite cold, especially at that morning hour. Soon, the Sanyasi was thumping his way to the school near which he had found accommodation. As he turned into the alley, he was amazed to see a palanquin that stood at the entrance; its pallbearers too stood nearby. He found his teacher, Swami Virajanand, in the courtyard. He hurriedly squatted before the teacher to touch his feet. Blessing in reply, he said, "Come on, lead me to the palanquin. And you have to follow me."

The Sanyasi held the blind Sage's hand and helped him into the palanquin. As the pallbearers took it up on their shoulders and set off, he accompanied the four pupils who also followed. Soon, the party turned off the paved path to move on the dusty, narrow walkway along the Yamuna. The forest started soon. Having gone for about a mile, they arrived at a clearing. An ordinary shamiana was already there with quite a few people. The Sanyasi felt that his Guru was being received very warmly, as if he were an important person.

It is said that this meeting had been inspired by Virajanand. The way it was being conducted in the dense forest it ought to be a secret mission. This event is mentioned only in one place. Its details were recorded in Urdu by Mir Mushtaq Meerasi, a representative of the Central Office (Sorem) of the Sarvakhap Panchayat (the organisation of all Khaps or village groups) and filed in its office. This report is recorded in a book, published by Arya Prakashan, and written by Pindidas Jnani.

Meerasi writes in this report that a Panchayat (assembly) was held in the forest of the pilgrimage town of Mathura in the month of Bhadrapad in 1856. He writes:

> "This Panchayat was attended by Nana Saheb Peshwa, Azimulla Khan and others in addition to the representatives of numerous Panchayats and landlords. Among other names were also included those of Ranga Babu and a prince of the Mughal emperor Bahadur Shah Zafar. All having been seated, a Hindu faqir was brought in a palanquin. All those present welcomed this Dervish [an ascetic monk]."

Adding further details, he says that this meeting went on for four days. On the first day, all guests were introduced to one another. On the second day, the Muslim scholars discussed religion. On the third day, the Hindu scholars discussed Rama, Krishna, Buddha and Shankaracharya, as well as other hermits, kings and emperors. Swami Virajanand was welcomed on the fourth day. In his address, he spoke on a variety of topics, of which those pertaining to the Uprising were more important. In his report, Meerasi states that only important people were allowed to be present on the fourth day, and any person related to the government was barred from attending it. The following quote explains the eminence that Swami Virajanand enjoyed:

> "When Mahatma [great soul] Virajanand was brought in a palanquin, the Hindu-Muslim faqirs played *Shankh* [shell], *Khadtal* [a percussion instrument], *Nagfani* [a wind instrument], *Nakkara* [a percussion drum], *Turahi* [a bugle-like wind instrument] and *Narsinghe* [trumpet] and sang in honour of God and nation. This priceless Sanyasi possessed the power to understand each atrocity and divine aura

reflected in his speech. I too spoke what I had to and then presented five flowers before him, bowed before him and prayed to God that such godly souls ought always be created for the well-being of the universe."

Using imagination, we would attempt to describe what transpired there. It was determined in this assembly that the Kamal Abhiyan or lotus campaign and the Chapati Abhiyan or flatbread campaign would continue unabated as before, and the date for the Revolution would be fixed as May 31, 1857. It was planned that all prominent cantonments would be infiltrated in order to incite the sepoys. The points on which they could be excited were also discussed. The chief speaker on this day was none other than Swami Virajanand. The Sanyasi sat nearby and listened to him attentively. The more he heard, the more respect he felt for him. Despite his sightless eyes, he possessed a very extensive foresight. He presented the entire plan as if he had seen all those places himself.

Having appointed representatives for all cantonments and towns, the only garrison town left was that of Meerut. Azimulla Khan intimated that no spy could as yet be appointed for Meerut, as the native sepoys and European soldiers were almost equal in number there, and as the Topkhana (magazine) was under English control, it made them very powerful, so it would be impossible to cause an uprising there.

"We are here to turn the impossible into possible," said Swami Virajanand as his words exuded his natural confidence and flamboyance.

"How can you say so?"

"This will be accomplished by my new pupil," said the elderly Guru, beckoning to his new pupil. All eyes turned towards him, yet the Sanyasi was thinking how Guruji knew where he sat. He had a divine vision for sure. His faith in his teacher was growing fathomless.

The Sanyasi had already started to think in his heart how he was going to execute the plan when he saw that a tall and sturdy man sitting next to him pressed his hand. He looked at him questioningly.

The fair man in a white dhoti-kurta appeared impressive with the slender smile that he wore on his lips. He said softly, "*Meerut mein thara Swagat hai.* (Thou are welcome in Meerut.)"

"Your introduction?" The Sanyasi was not fluent in Hindi. He was born in Gujarat, and the use of the word '*thara*' (thine) for himself had not made him feel any good.

"I am Shahmal, from Baraut in Meerut. It appears we will work together," he said in his rustic dialect. The Sanyasi at once realised that he appeared to be a useful guy and must be a representative of the local Khap. The man continued, "No problem would come across you, just call whenever you need anything."

The gathering also included more people from the Meerut region. With so many people around, the Sanyasi had come to believe that the dream of the Revolution could materialise substantially. In the assembly, he also saw a representative of Swami Purnanand, whom he had met in Haridwar. He approached him and murmured a message for his master that *he* had ultimately complied with what Swamiji wished.

***

In the evening, back in school, Swami Virajanand sent for the new disciple and asked him to sit near him. The Sanyasi was yet full of questions about how he would have to undertake his mission. Finally, he said, "What do I need to do at Meerut?"

"What have you heard at the meeting?" Swami Virajanand

possessed a somewhat strict demeanour. "You have to incite the sepoys, what else?"

"How do I start?"

"You have to chart your way yourself."

"Is it so simple a task to meet the sepoys?"

"No, not at all. You will select a den quite in or near the cantonment, all the better if the sepoys visit the place. A religious place can serve this purpose, but the choice remains yours. There will be people to help you out. No more questions. The brave march on their own. You are brave, so I believe. Act as you find the situation there."

The Sanyasi's resolve reflected in his eyes. He said, "I will sacrifice even my life to abide by your bidding."

"No, I need you. You need to know what Chhatrapati Shivaji told Chhatrasal when he uttered words like yours. He said that by sacrificing yourself, you earn glory for yourself, but the nation's cause is left unfulfilled. Same for you. You have to just accomplish your goal and move out. We have a higher goal before ourselves that has to be accomplished, that alone would make the nation truly free. I don't like to repeat things. Can you understand?"

"I just need to ask a couple of things, if you permit."

"Hmm!"

"What are these Kamal Abhiyan and Chapati Abhiyan?"

Virajanand described these campaigns in detail. The assembly came to a close. The next day, the Sanyasi had to set off towards his destination. This time, he would not be on foot, nor would he be alone; many other people would accompany him. He was about to undertake a historic mission, but he had clear instructions from his teacher to remain nameless, anonymous, unknown. To achieve the superior goal, the lower glory could be forgone.

5: Prior Planning and Campaigns

Several historians opine that the 1857 Uprising was a spontaneous event. There are, however, several pieces of evidence that confirm its prior planning. During the course of this book, the incidences of preplanning at different levels would keep coming up. How the British viewed the Uprising, whether it was planned or not, the views of the historian Arthur D. Annes, in his book *A Short History of the British in India*, appear quite rational:

> "The truth has to be found somewhere between those who say that the Revolt was simply a Mutiny of sepoys in a panic, and those who call the Mutiny an organized Revolt. The panic was engineered by political intriguers, but the insurrection was not organized. . .There is every indication that the sepoys took their first leap blindly in the dark, not knowing whether they were going. But there is also every indication that the Nana Saheb on the one side and a Mogul faction on the other had a great deal to do with working them up to take the leap. . ."

There are numerous facts that point to the Chapati and Lotus Campaigns, two clandestine but much-discussed ones. Both of them started in the early months of the revolution year; however, there is some concrete evidence that points to the preparation much earlier than these. It would be incumbent upon us to discuss them first.

Among the foremost heroes of the 1857 Uprising is the name of Kunwar Singh, a landlord of Jagdishpur, Bihar. He had started to make preparations for this Uprising almost 11- 12 years prior to its actual eruption. In the Punjab, there spread unruliness after the death of Maharaja Ranjit Singh in 1839. The English decided to take advantage of this situation as they were already on a spree to grab more territories. This interference resulted in two wars, the first of which occurred in 1845-46. Learning a vital lesson from the English strategy, the elderly Kunwar Singh decided to use their very trick against them. At that time, the English army and resources were pinned down in the Punjab. He thought that the Sikhs should be rendered assistance, and at the same time, a foundation for the uprising in Bihar should be laid. To realise this dual purpose, he sought help from other landlords and Taluqdars, besides arranging money to be used for inciting the sepoys garrisoned at Danapur Cantonment (near Patna). He was also desirous of seeking assistance from the Nepalese King, then facing upheaval in politics.

Unfortunately, this plan was revealed to the English officers at Patna that money was being distributed among military officers and sepoys of Danapur. In this connection, one Rahat Ali was arrested too. The enquiry revealed that several influential people, landlords and jagirdars (they were often called Rajahs or kings) had convened an assembly at Haribar Chhattar on the occasion of Sonepur Fair, in which a plan was set afoot to constitute fighting bands at several places, including at Jagdishpur. It was also decided to seek assistance from Nepal and the Mughal ruler in Delhi. These people were assigned the task of spreading disaffection among native sepoys at different places, which included Danapur, Sigauli (Sugauli), Hazaribagh (now in Jharkhand) and Daronda (now in Jharkhand), among others. The Commissioner of Patna, William Tayler, refers to this plot in these words in his book *Our Crisis*, as quoted by John Kaye:

> "...for some years past, this city [Patna] has been considered a very sink of disaffection and intrigue. In 1846, a dangerous plot was detected, in which many of the Mohamadens of Patna and neighbouring districts were concerned and in which attempts had been made to tamper with the sepoys."

Elphinstone Jackson, the magistrate of Shahabad, under which Jagdishpur fell then, wrote to the Secretary to the Government of Bengal, on January 3, 1846:

> "I have received letters containing the information that Babu Koer Singh, a most influential zamindar of this district and a man most highly popular with all the inhabitants of Arrah and other towns of Shahabad, is suspected of being leagued with the conspirators and that letters bearing his seal have been discovered proving his guilt."

The historian K.K. Datta, in his book *Unrest Against the British Rule in Bihar 1831-1859*, published in 1917, writes that the work of forming an army at Jagdishpur under the command of Kunwar Singh had already commenced.

In this connection, the then Commissioner EC Ravenshaw had warned the Governor General and had raids conducted at several places. In Patna itself, a parcel was recovered from a well located in the house of one Malik Kadam Ali, which was secured in bricks and a floormat, inside of which were found papers in a piece of bamboo. These papers had got wet, so they were dried up, and an effort was made to read them with a magnifying glass.

Most of these were letters written by Kunwar Singh to Khwaja Hussain Ali, Kadam Ali, Barakatulla, etc., and they bore his seal too. Patna's Magistrate already possessed evidence against him that he was in contact with Rahat Ali; he had sent a messenger to Nepal; and that he was in command of several activities being undertaken against the British Raj. It was also revealed that

Kunwar Singh would lead an army to Lahore to take part in the ongoing Anglo-Sikh war. Yet another letter revealed that funds for the operation had been arranged, but it was unclear whether they had been delivered to him. Looking at all these proofs, Patna's Magistrate wrote to Shahabad's Magistrate to conduct an enquiry against Kunwar Singh and to arrest him.

The English often took horrendous retaliatory action even on the slightest suspicion. So far as this case was concerned, it is, however, amazing to note that Kunwar Singh was not even summoned for interrogation, let alone arresting him. This entails the power and influence that this elderly warrior wielded. Its cause has been mentioned by the English themselves. Shahabad's Magistrate Elphinstone Jackson, in his letter to the Secretary to the Government of Bengal, said that the arrest of Babu Kunwar Singh would force the people to rise in revolt who follow his orders, and the consequences would be fatal. The English had realised that any such action against Kunwar Singh would amount to rendering the entire province restless, and in addition to the people of Nepal and Shahabad, they would also have to deal with the zamindars and Rajahs of Tikri, Gaya, Sasaram, Darbhanga, Betia, Hutwa and other places, all of whom were being aided by government officials, moneylenders and traders.

It would also be worth noting that the English officers knew full well that Khwaja Hussain (Hasan) Ali was the leader of this entire episode, so his arrest was attempted, but to no avail. Even more interesting is the fact that Khwaja surrendered himself before Patna's Magistrate, but he had to be set free a couple of days later, on October 27, 1846. Thus, in the entire conspiracy, neither arrest nor punishment happened. Of course, as a face-saving device, two native sepoys were awarded minor punishments—Durga Prasad Pandit to be incarcerated for three years' imprisonment and Jemadar Beekhan Khan to be discharged from service. Kaye termed this occurrence as the 'forecast of the imminent tempest'.

To transform this 'tempest' into reality, Kunwar Singh was once again planning at the beginning of 1856. This time, he wished that the planned outbreak would spread through the entire country simultaneously. He once again contacted the Taluqdars, zamindars, and Rajahs of Bihar and Awadh. Wake, the Magistrate of Arrah, wrote to Patna's Commissioner on January 29, 1858:

> "...the information I have received leaves no room for doubt that Koer Singh had for some time been planning the rebellion and was waiting for Dinapur [Danapur] Regiments."

He also mentions in his letter a petition, written by an anonymous person and forwarded by Wake to the Commissioner, "detailing the whole of the Baboo's [Babu Kunwar Singh's] plans and preparations and even the exact date [25th of July) on which the Dinapur Regiment would mutiny. This was forwarded by me, I think, a week before the Mutiny, and every word of it proved true".

In 1855, an anonymous long letter was written to the (British) Government of Bengal, warning it of the evil consequences of the British atrocities. It was then sent as an enclosure to the Commissioners of Patna and Bhagalpur Divisions on October 8, 1855. Among other things, the letter also said:

> "The people of Hindoostan would wish to fight before schools are established and Musjeeds [mosques] of the Mahomadens and the temples of the Hindoos, destroyed. Accordingly, the Zamindars and Rajahs of Muzaffarpore [Muzaffarpur], Arrah, Chupra [Chhapra], Azimabad, Sahebganj and Bhaugalpore [Bhagalpur], and the sepoys attached to the jails and Collectorates of these districts, have formed themselves into a party, one of whom has been

> deputed to the Rajah of Putteallah [Patiala], one to the Santhals and other to the Rajah of Nepal and to Emperor of Delhi."

In 1856, when the English had attached Awadh on false grounds of mismanagement and Nawab Wajid Ali Shah was pensioned off to Calcutta, he had met the revolutionaries at Kanpur and Patna. Dr. K.K. Datta has quoted Subedar Hidayat Ali of the Native Sikh Infantry who has written that "on 24 March [1856] when the Nawab of Lucknow also arrived there, enroute to Calcutta, the chief persons of the city, the Vakeel of the Raja of Bithur and the Officers and the Sepoys from the regiments stationed there used to pay visits to the Vakeels and servants of the Nawab".

In a like manner, the Nawab had met the Muslim leaders at Patna too when he stopped there overnight. Patna's Commissioner Tayler has written:

> "It was previously within my knowledge that when the King of Oude passed through Patna, Mehdee Ali, the Cotegusht or Patrol Daroga of this city, who is a man of superior knowledge and attainments, resident of Lucknow, had been frequently admitted into the royal presence and was treated with the greatest consideration."

Even during his sojourn in Calcutta, the Nawab remained in contact with the revolutionaries. This was why he was imprisoned soon after the Uprising broke out.

In March 1857, a proclamation was posted on the walls of the Jama Masjid and in surrounding areas in Delhi stating that a Persian army would soon arrive to free India from the English. On it was written the name of one Muhammad Sadiq, but no one knew who he was. Kaye, in Vol. 2, has mentioned one Mukund Lal, secretary to the Mughal ruler, reporting that the personal attendants of the Mughal ruler conversed with one another that the army would soon revolt and enter the palace to place the Mughal ruler on the throne.

Nana Saheb had undertaken several journeys across North India a few months before the eruption. John Kaye notes in his Vol. I that he had visited several places in the months leading up to the Uprising, including Delhi, where he is likely to have visited Meerut as well.

In addition to the above incidents, the prior planning also included the Kamal (or Lotus) and Chapati (or Flatbread) Campaigns. It would be pertinent to know more about them. Several writers have described them in varying detail.

In 1857, the Company was about to complete a century of its rule. The English planned to hold a large celebration to mark this occasion. This plan was yet in the conception stage when the Chapati Campaign took off in the Agra and Awadh region and spread to a wider area. It was in two forms. In the first, a saint or faqir would divide and distribute a chapati among people. The people who got this as Prasad would roll more chapatis at home to distribute them to the others. This Prasad also accompanied a message against the English. The village headman, too, was given a chapati, which he would distribute among his villagers. Also, he would bake five more chapatis to send one each to the adjoining villages.

The extent of the Chapati Campaign can be known from the report of Major Erskine, commissioner of Sagar and Narmada region (now in Madhya Pradesh):

> "So far back as January 1857, small wheaten cakes [chapatis] were passed in a most mysterious manner from village to village in most of the districts. . ."

> Likewise, Captain Keatinge has noted:

> "The year 1857 opened in Nimar by general distribution of

> small cakes, which were passed on from village to village. The same, I am aware, has occurred all over Northern India, and has been spoken of as having been a signal for the disturbances which took place later in the year."

There is also an accompanying rumour about these chapatis that messages were annotated on them. Kaye notes in Volume 1 of his book:

> "Some, too, surmised that, by a device sometimes used for other purposes, seditious letters were in this manner forwarded from village to village, read by the village chief, again crusted over with flour, and sent on in the shape of a chupatty, to be broken by the next recipient. But whatsoever the history of the movement, it had doubtless the effect of producing and keeping alive much popular excitement in the districts through which the cakes were transmitted; and it may be said that its action was too widely diffused, and that it lasted for too long a time. . ."

The book '*The Revelations of an Orderly*' (published in 1866), written by an orderly named Paunchkowree Khan, contains his views about the English administration. It describes how the prisoners were delivered vital information with food, and a similar methodology was likely adopted elsewhere:

> "Suppose a prisoner is confined under the bayonet of Sepoys, he must be permitted to eat bread. The preparer of the food is bribed, and a short note is put into a chupatty, or a sentence is written on a plate, and when the bread is taken up the prisoner reads what is written."

The other form of the Chapati Campaign was more terrible. In it, under the cover of darkness, four or five chapatis were placed on the work table of an English officer in his office. The English tried their best to find out how the chapatis reached there, but to no avail. No head or tail of the campaign could be ascertained. The Company employees were terrorised as this expressed the inner anger of the native people. The intelligence department also failed to find a clue. Rumours were the order of the day. It was also said that these chapatis travelled 150-200 miles a night.

The Kamal or Lotus Campaign, too, was operational simultaneously, with the difference that while the Chapati Campaign was run among common folks, the Kamal Campaign was conducted among prominent people such as rulers, Rajas, zamindars, and village headmen. When one of them received a lotus, he was expected to send at least five fresh lotuses to other people.

Maybe these campaigns were initiated in January 1857. How they started has several legends. According to one, Nana Saheb often visited the monastery of Dasbuva at Bithur. When the English, under the Doctrine of Lapse, decided not to approve Nana Saheb's pension and title, he, being the adopted son of the last Peshwa of the Maratha empire, set out to plan an armed outbreak. Once when he visited the monastery, he explained his plight to the ascetic Dasbuva, who, in response, picking out some baked chapatis from the fireplace and gathering a few lotuses offered to the sacred image there, gave them to Nana Saheb with the words: "Spread them, the extent to which they reach will form part of your kingdom."

Another legend holds that the Lotus Campaign was initiated by Maulvi Ahamadulla Shah of Faizabad (Ayodhya).

From the above discussion, it becomes evident that the massive revolution of 1857 was not a spontaneous occurrence; instead, monumental efforts went into it. Writing Indian history poses a significant challenge, especially given the lack of evidence. The period we are writing about was the one in which Indians wrote little, due to which there prevails an absence of circumstantial facts and proofs. The chapati and lotus campaigns are supported mainly by a few statements from the British. Similarly, the sole evidence about the jungle meeting at Mathura can well be doubted in the absence of corroboration. However, there is no shortage of indirect evidence about them all. Can't we accept our traditional culture, folktales, and folksongs as evidence? The established practice for them is that they should be corroborated with concrete evidence, but in a case like this, we can certainly accept them as sources, as they are founded in some actual event; of course, not without a pinch of salt, as they might be somewhat exaggerated.

When we corroborate the concrete evidence with popular beliefs and traditional literature, the foggy atmosphere starts to clear out, from which emerges the bright panoramic view, which acts as a source of boundless energy in the dormant bodies, arousing the sublime spirit of patriotism in which scores of people sacrificed their lives without a second thought.

Note: It's a coincidence that two of the three greatest warriors of the 1857 Uprising, as determined by several British writers, including Malleson, have found a mention in this chapter: Veer Kunwar Singh of Jagdishpur and Maulvi Ahamadulla Shah of Faizabad. The third one is Tatya Tope, who fought alongside Nana Saheb and Rani Lakshmibai of Jhansi, and was mentioned earlier in the book.

6: The Land of Revolution

Before we speak of the campaign at Meerut, it would be better to understand the geography of Meerut Cantonment to understand better the events related to the Uprising.

Well-known as Krantidhara, or the Land of Revolution, Meerut is an important district in the western region of Uttar Pradesh and contributes to the country's economy in more fields than one. With traces of the Ramayana and Mahabharata eras, the district has carved out a distinct place for itself in the country. Located between the Ganga and the Yamuna, the land has been formed from the silt brought by these two great rivers and their tributaries. As water is abundant, expansive greenery has found its vibrant empire in the region. The climate here allows growing two or three crops a year.

In 1857, the district of Meerut comprised the area now forming part of the present-day districts of Baghpat, Ghaziabad and Hapur in addition to the parent district, and two tehsils of Gautam Buddha Nagar (Noida). According to the Meerut Gazetteer, in 1853 the district covered 2362 square miles and had a population of 11,35,072. The number of villages in it was 1373; of which, 1077 villages had fewer than 1000 people, 288 had between 1000 and 5000 people, and 8 had more than 5000 people each. The district, with a vast area and abundant resources, was close to Delhi and attracted the British, who took it under their control in 1803 after they clasheded with the Marathas. They set up the cantonment here in 1806.

In 1857, the Mughal empire was in rapid decline, with Bahadur Shah Zafar serving only as a titular head. Over the past few decades, the Mughals were under the subordination of the Marathas and other invaders, and now the English were their masters. Presently, Zafar was incapable of doing anything without English approval. Owing to such upheaval, the law-and-order situation was growing from bad to worse. At this time, the city of Meerut was located mostly within a fort with seven approaches or gates, some of which can still be seen today, but there is no trace of the boundary wall. The English set up the cantonment in the city's eastern, northern, and western directions.

Quite in the middle of the cantonment flowed the nullah, known as Abu Ka Nala, whose water was then used for drinking; today it has been reduced to a drain carrying wastewater. In the northern part of this nullah, facilities were created for the European populace, which included bungalows, a church, a cemetery, a theatre, cinemas, Mall Road, clubs, a Company Garden, schools, a Topkhana (artillery magazine) and others. To the southern side of the nullah were erected barracks, messes, etc., for the native troops. A few bungalows and other facilities were also created on this side for European officers serving in the native regiments.

If you look at these two parts, the biased, racist attitude of the English becomes quite obvious. The Indians were not allowed in places like Company Garden (now rechristened Gandhi Bagh), Mall Road and other facilities in the northern part, and there were placed billboards saying: "Indians and Dogs Not Allowed." They will have to bear with the consequences of such prejudice and racism, and now is the time to rise against the injustice.

To meet the ration and other needs, a main market called Sadar Bazar was established in the cantonment to the south of the nullah. A market called Abu Lane was also developed along the nullah; today, it is considered an elite market. There were (and are) two main parts of Sadar Bazar: a wholesale market from which large quantities of rations for the army were procured, and the other, a retail market that catered to small-scale personal needs. Unlike today, the army lacked a supply corps, so most goods were procured from local markets. This is one reason that in each important cantonment, a Sadar Bazar was also established. The retail market remained crowded, often on Sundays and holidays. This was the market that would incubate the Uprising, the one that would root out the Company Raj. Near the market was also established a police station; another, called Kotwali, was located within the walled city.

It would be adequate to have an estimate of the army's strength here. In all other cantonments across India, the number of native sepoys far exceeded that of the European troops; it was only at Meerut that the balance of strength favoured the Europeans. In May 1857, there were three native and three English regiments. Of the native regiments, two were infantry (11th and 20th), and one was cavalry (3rd), with a total of 2234 native sepoys; all three were located to the south of the nullah. In comparison, the English regiments included one infantry (the first battalion of 60th King's Royal Rifles), one cavalry (6th Dragoon Guard) equipped with horse-drawn field guns, and one artillery magazine, with the total number of European troops at 1778; all of them posted to the north of the nullah. Besides, 123 native sepoys were posted in the artillery who lived nearby.

The European troops numbered slightly fewer than the native counterparts, but with the artillery under their control, they were very powerful. This was one reason why the English never felt threatened that an uprising could ever start at Meerut, as was the case with other cantonments like Kanpur. The fact remains that it was here that all this began and quickly spread through the breadth and length of the country.

The Sanyasi had already entered Meerut and was engaged in undertaking the work assigned to him. He was now looking for a suitable place to settle down for his purpose.

7: Bracing up for Action

Our protagonist, the Sanyasi, is said to have first set out from Mathura for Ambala, and from there he turned to Meerut. It was about January in the year 1857. There was no sensation of the controversial cartridge in the air. The Sanyasi went round the cantonment to find a suitable place to stay. Unlike the bygone years, he was not alone either.

For about two months, he kept working in different parts of the district, building a chain of people, assigning tasks to his comrades, motivating them, and spreading rumours. He provided momentum to the Lotus Campaign and the Chapati Campaign, too. He knew well that, even if the sepoys revolted, the Uprising could not be sustained without active support from the civilian populace. The way this team succeeded in sowing apprehension among common folks could be seen in the consistent rumours in other districts that Meerut had risen in revolt. The prevailing state of excitement in Meerut can be gauged from John Kaye's words:

> "With vague but eager expectancy, the Native regiments at all the large stations in Upper India were looking in that [Meerut's] direction, as for a signal which they knew would soon be discerned. Men asked each other what was the news from Mirath, and looked into the native newspapers for the suggestive heading; for it was the cradle of all sorts of strange and disturbing stories. . . Every day the excitement increased, for every day some new story, intended to confirm the popular belief in the base designs of the English, found its way into circulation."

Towards the close of March, the Sanyasi was in search of an adequate place in the cantonment. He spotted a monastery near the new jail. There were two jails in Meerut at that time—one at Kesarganj and the other in the cantonment, where Victoria Park (Bhamashah Park) is today. The latter was under the Company's army, and a few native sepoys were posted here as well. Now, no trace of this jail remains. Suraj Kund is located quite near this park; it is a historical place where Hindus cremate the dead. A monastery was then located just outside Suraj Kund. Today, a beautiful temple exists in this monastery, called Baba Manoharnath Temple.

In the Topkhana or magazine located nearby, only 123 native sepoys were posted, who were not even required to use the cartridge. A handful more, from the 20th Native Infantry Regiment, were posted at the new jail. These sepoys and others visited the monastery for daily rituals. The rumour about the greased cartridge had already made its way to Meerut, but these sepoys could not be excited about this ground; so the Sanyasi was not very happy with the place and was looking for an alternative site for himself where he could be in contact with a larger number of sepoys. He was doing his bit, yet he doubted his success. What he intended was to cause a frightening flare to rise. That, however, could not be feasible because the number of native sepoys in this part of the cantonment was small, while the European soldiers numbered far more. So, he was looking actively for an alternative place where he could accomplish his task with a better chance of success.

Common folks also visited this monastery. The Sanyasi would often explain religion in reference to patriotism. Every evening, an assembly was held, during which religious and patriotic songs were sung. In Hinduism, both concepts are accepted as complementary. Whatever the topic he spoke about, he would invariably quote the English prejudice, atrocity and exploitation in one or the other way. He would continue the Chapati Campaign, distributing chapatis among visitors, and often made them vow to hold the national pride high when the opportunity arose. Despite his lack of command of Hindi, let alone the local dialect Khari Boli, his preaching style was interesting, and he grew popular in the area, leading to an increase in visitors. This, however, had an adverse impact too. In just a few days, the administration grew suspicious of his activities, and the district magistrate ordered him to quit the district. Kaye describes him in these words:

> "The emissary of evil, who, in some shape or another, was stalking across the country, was at Mirath in the guise of a wandering Fakir, or religious mendicant, riding on an elephant, with many followers. That he was greatly disturbing the minds of men was certain; so the Police authorities ordered him to depart. He moved, but it was believed that he went no farther than the Lines of one of the Native regiments."

The *Mirath Narratives*, written by Williams, Commissioner First Division, reveal why the Sanyasi was asked to move out:

> "The frequent visits of the men of the Native regiments to him attracted attention, and he was ordered, through the police, to leave the place; he apparently complied, but, it is said, he stayed some time in the Lines of the 20th Native Infantry."

A similar description appears in Savarkar's book. The *Meerut Gazetteer* has described him in these words:

> "Early in April, an emissary in the guise of a Hindu faqir, riding on an elephant and attended by a few horsemen and a number of native carriages, came into the city and was visited by several of the native troops. He was ordered

> to leave the station but is said to have been for some time concealed in the lines of the 20th Native Infantry."

It was inevitable that the Sanyasi quit the place to avoid any police action against him, which could render his entire plan useless. The beginning of April 1857 brought news that could help him realise his intention: the new cartridge and how native sepoys in some regiments elsewhere were being forced to use it. His entire plan was on the brink of failure due to this order. He asked the police officer for a couple of days' leave to move away. During the evening assembly, he shared his problem with the sepoys.

This order provided him with a golden opportunity. He was advised that there was a small temple with an Aughardani (Shivlinga), with a well nearby, very near the 20th Native Regiment. As the well was the source of water for the regiment, both Hindu and Muslim sepoys visited it regularly, and it could be a suitable place for him. Today, this place is Meerut's most famous shrine, known as Baba Augharnath Temple. Acharya Dipankar has written in his Hindi book, *Swadhinata Andolan aur Meerut* (*Freedom Struggle and Meerut*), that this Sanyasi, known as Aughar Baba, stayed here, after whom it has acquired its present name. As the British, called the native troops 'Kala' or 'Kali' (black), it became more popular as the Kali Paltan Temple. Today, it is a splendid temple with a large area. It has become a popular spot on Mondays and on all Hindu festivals. Each year in the month of Shravan (July-August), lakhs of Kanwariyas or religious pilgrims bring water from the Ganga at Haridwar or further up from the river's origin, Gangotri, to offer to Lord Shiva here.

The Sanyasi also realised that suspicion about him rose due to the number of followers, horses, elephants and carriages he had, so he decided to be there all alone and sent the remaining followers away to work in the countryside, who joined the wandering mendicants, faqirs and *madaris* (street jugglers) who were already doing their bidding. Several writers have written about these wandering people. Dr Nidhi Sharma has pointed this out in her book titled *1857*. Savarkar writes in his book:

> "Hundreds of emissaries in the garb of faqirs and hermits were busy propagating at different places. As approaching households in the name of seeking alms was convenient without raising an iota of doubt in the enemy's mind, these patriotic faqirs and hermits went from door to door to spread hatred against slavery and cultivate ambition in the communities."

The Sanyasi was in touch with merely two hundred sepoys at Suraj Kund, but at this new place, he was able to establish contact with the sepoys of all three native regiments, as they all were located close by. In the monastery, the sepoys visited him only in the evening; while here, the sepoys kept coming the whole day to draw water from the well. More importantly, most of the sepoys visiting the monastery were from the artillery, who did not need to use muskets or rifles, whereas these sepoys had muskets and rifles as their main weapons. Most of the time, the Sanyasi would draw water for the visiting sepoys and offer it to them, engaging them in his convincing talks. He would tell them that a handful of Englishmen had occupied the whole of India because of them. While the English enjoyed due to their hard work, they got peanuts. He would rub their wounds with salt, that they got neither money nor respect. He would say that they were the instruments that killed the countrymen to fill the foreigners' coffers. And now he owned an effective formula to excite the sepoys' minds – the greased cartridge.

Before we proceed, it is important to understand what the greased cartridge was and the travails and troubles it brought.

8: The First Spark

A Brahmin sepoy, after his bath in the river, was walking back to his barrack with a water-filled *lota* (a metal water pot with a curved mouth) in his hand. On the way, he met a *khalasi* (a low-class worker) who asked him for water. The sepoy chided him, "Keep away, if you touch my *lota*, it will be defiled. You wish to pollute my faith, don't you?"

"Now defilement would envelop around," said the *khalasi* in a taunting tone.

"What do you mean?" The sepoy stood bewildered.

"The cartridges…that you are going to tear off with your mouth," said the *khalasi* before walking away, "are all soaked in cow and hog fat."

These words caused a tempest in the sepoy's heart. The *khalasi*, believed to be named Matadin Hela, never knew how deeply his words were going to hurt. The historians claim that his wife, Lajo, a handmaid in an English officer's house, had informed him of the use of fat in pouches meant to envelope the cartridges to prevent them from drying.

The caste system continues to be rooted deep in India even today; in those days, the glorious Varna system of ancient times had degraded into the rigid caste system, in which untouchability was at its zenith. This minor incident occurred at Dumdum (now in West Bengal); however, no one realised it could have such massive repercussions. The well-known historians Sir John Kaye and Malleson, in their book *Indian Mutiny of 1857-8* (Vol. 1), describe this occurrence in these words:

> "Now, it happened that, one day in January, a low-caste Lascar, or magazine-man, meeting a high-caste Sipahi in the Cantonment, asked him for a drink of water from his lotah. The Brahman [Brahmin] at once replied with an objection on the score of caste, and was tauntingly told that caste was nothing, that high-caste and low-caste would soon be all the same, as cartridges smeared with beef-fat and hog's-lard were being made for the Sipahis at the depots, and would soon be in general use throughout the army."

When the Khalasi was asked to prove his claim, he is said to have taken the sepoy to the magazine where the cartridges were being packed, and he saw 50-60 people applying grease to the pouches.

***

Since their arrival in India, the British had conducted several studies of the people here. Many of these studies were written down at the Company's behest, and the chosen ones formed part of the District Gazetteers. Besides, several other European writers have written in detail about contemporary events. All these prove vital but prejudiced sources of history. Not only this, policies were formulated based on these studies, and lacunae in India's social systems, like the caste system, as well as strong points like the native education and family (cottage) industrial system, were exploited to their advantage and later formulated their well-known policy of 'divide and rule' so as to perpetuate their rule.

Their studies and interactions with the native populace revealed that Indians, by nature, were obedient and loyal, so they could be relied on as workers and soldiers. This was one reason why the Company recruited a large number of them for its army. The Company's policies had put pressure on native agriculture and cottage industry, forcing people to seek work outside their familial vocations. Employment with the Company, especially recruitment in the army, had emerged as a major source of employment; it had also attained social prestige, as it ensured a stable income amidst the prevailing instability. The English, therefore, felt that the Indians would never rise against them.

Despite this, a number of uprisings had occurred even before 1857. These resistances were usually small and regional. The English confronted one such small-scale sepoys' uprising in 1824, when the 47th Regiment at Barrackpore refused to proceed to Burma; it was disbanded in retaliation. In 1844, the sepoys acquiesced to going to Sindh only when the foreign service allowance, called 'batta', was paid to them; the Company had to submit to the demand. The largest number of uprisings occurred during the governor-generalship of Lord Dalhousie; three of the prominent ones were in 1848, 1849, and 1852; of course, all of them were crushed rather easily. These uprisings were other than those which were started by farmers, zamindars and jagirdars (landlords), and tribals like Santhals and Kols, and others.

Of all the uprisings prior to 1857, the largest was that of Vellore, in Madras province in South India (now Tamil Nadu). In 1806, the sepoys occupied the fort at Vellore for a day, inflicting 200 casualties on the European soldiers and officers. The English were forced to summon an army from Arcot (Carnatic, now Karnataka). In the resultant conflict, more than 100 native sepoys were captured, lined along a wall and shot in cold blood.

The English ought to have learnt a lesson from the cause of this resistance; however, in half a century, they seemed to have erased it from their memory, which could have cost them the fort, and maybe had larger implications for their fledgling empire at the time. This cause was disrespect to the religious sentiments of the native populace and biased treatment based on racism.

In November 1805, General Sir John Caddock, commander-in-chief of the Madras Army, issued an order that the Hindu sepoys would not be able to daub their traditional *Tilak* on their foreheads, while the Muslims would have to clean-shave themselves. The sepoys felt unhappy with this. The Indian sepoys wore a turban in those days. Now, they were to wear a round hat, a type of hat worn by Europeans and natives converted to Christianity. This hat was also fixed with a leather badge. The native sepoys had no objection to wearing leather belts, shoes and the like, but they were unwilling to wear leather on the head, which was a cause of their discontent.

In the fort of Vellore resided the descendants and other relatives, including wives and sons, of Tipu, the Sultan of Mysore, who died fighting the English just seven years ago in 1799. On the occasion of a girl's wedding in the family, the sepoys garrisoned there broke out in a revolution. They demanded that Tipu's son should be declared the ruler of Mysore. It is conjectured that these descendants were part of the conspiracy; however, there is every reason to doubt the veracity of this claim, as they refused to lead the disaffected sepoys.

By 1857, the English appeared to have forgotten that intervention in religious values could prove costly. Over time, they had grown habituated to undermining the natives' religious sentiments. Speaking about the malevolent intention of the British officers, Arthur D. Annes has, in his book *A Short History of the British in India*, written:

> "There were always a few British officers who were far too ready to override religious prejudices in their disciplinary regulations. Of recent years, missionaries had been allowed to become more aggressive. The Government had put down

> the practice of suttee [Sati custom], and had refused to let a change of religion interfere with inheritance as the Hindu Law prescribed."

The act they were about to commit, however, would prove detrimental to their interests and lives. This was the introduction of the new cartridges. Almost all historians have attributed the Revolution to the controversial greased cartridge. About this time, the groundwork for the Revolution was being laid in several places across India. Effectively, the new cartridge had set off a spark in the gunpowder that was already there, whose presence had been caused by the English through their policies and the active efforts of certain Indian revolutionaries. Vinayak Damodar Savarkar, in his book on this Uprising, writes that the rumour that the cartridges were greased with fat only set fire to the explosive mines that several causes had created.

In the Company army, the old Brown Bess musket was yet in use. It was inconvenient to load, and its effective firepower was limited. In 1856, the Company decided to introduce a new rifle called the Enfield. It was first manufactured at Enfield, England, so it was named after the town. In India, it was now being manufactured in Ambala (presently in Haryana) and Dumdum, yet its nomenclature continued. It was more effective than the musket in use at the time. Its cartridge came packed in a paper pouch. To prevent the paper from drying up, grease was applied to it. To load, the gun was held in the left hand while the cartridge was inserted by the right hand; however, tearing off the pouch with one hand was not possible, so it was torn by squeezing it between the teeth. A rumour went around that the grease used in it was being mixed with the fat from cows and hogs. The cow is regarded as sacrosanct by the Hindus, while the hog (pig) is offensive to the Muslims. Thus, it was considered the cause of defiling their faiths.

Rising smoke can be a sure sign of a fire, as was the case with rumours. It is worth noting that on August 15, 1856, the Arsenal at Fort William entered into a contract with Gungadhur & Co. for the supply of 'Grease, Tallow' for two years at two annas per pound, for use in ammunition and rifle ammunition, respectively. Quoting this indent, Kaye writes in Volume 1 of his book:

> "So the cartridges manufactured for the Enfield rifles were to be smeared with a mixture of stearine and tallow. The Ordinance Department then indented for tallow, without any specification of the nature of the animal fat composing it; and, although no hog's lard was supplied, there is no question that some beef fat was used in the composition of the tallow."

It may be noted that of stearine and tallow in the above quote, stearin(e) is found in solid fat of some animals and vegetations, while 'tallow' can be fat from beef or sheep. The historian Surendranath Sen has, in his book *Eighteen Fifty-Seven*, quoted *The Times* dated February 23, 1857, thus:

> "The cartridges of the new Enfield rifle are greased at one end to make them slip readily into the barrel. The government ordered mutton fat for the purpose. Some contractors, to save a few shillings, gave pigs' and bullocks' fat instead."

The Inspector General of Ordnance at Fort William could give no assurance that the fat used was derived from unexceptional sources. The only defence he offered was that the tallow and grease were supplied by a Bengali Brahmin contractor, but that did not preclude the possibility that his men had supplied the cheapest material available in the market. Even the Englishmen believed that the contractor had supplied objectionable tallow since he was not specifically instructed to do otherwise. Kaye goes on to compare this with what had happened at Vellore in 1806:

> "Like the case of the leathern head-dresses which had convulsed Southern India half a century before, it appealed to the strongest feelings both of the Mahammadan and the Hindu; but though similar in kind, it was incomparably more offensive in degree; more insulting, more appalling, more disgusting."

The English seemed to be hiding the truth about these cartridges. An English officer admitted that fat from hogs or oxen was used in them. The *Meerut Gazetteer* clearly mentions that the rumour had spread not only among sepoys but also in the bazaars that the sepoys were to be issued cartridges greased with the controversial fat.

The Company had established its rule by brute force and trickery. Any admission of an unfair practice could be perceived as its weakness. Surendranath Sen writes:

> "Many [British] officers honestly felt that no allowance should be made for the sepoys' feelings and any concession might be construed as weakness. Hearsey [commander-in-chief at Barrackpore] tried his logic with his incredulous audience; individual sepoys and native officers were prosecuted and punished even for talking about the cartridge."

All this had sprouted from a rumour, yet it set deep down the sepoys' psyche. Even the English had come to know of what was going on in the sepoys' minds, yet they pretended to be ignorant of this. They called the natives 'heathen' which signified that they themselves belonged to a superior faith, while the Indians subordinate to them hailed from an irreligion or inferior faith. As their experience in America and Africa went, they felt that any person from any religion other than Christianity could be easily converted to their faith. Not only this, but active efforts were often made in this direction. When a regiment was not engaged in operations, the padres and missionaries were invited to deliver sermons.

The officers themselves did not lag in motivating (coercing) the sepoys to adopt Christianity, in reward for which they were promoted to the ranks of jemadar and subedar. It was widely believed that the English officers often held in one hand a promotion letter with a Bible on it. They, however, appeared to have overlooked the fact that the faiths of Hinduism and Islam enjoyed far deeper roots in India. Their culture was old and superior.

***

The rumour, emerging from the interaction between the Brahmin sepoy and the khalasi, spread like wildfire in Dumdum, then to Barrackpore, the headquarters of the Presidency division of the British Army, not far away. Now the sepoys grew suspicious of even the cartridges which they had been using in the Brown Bess musket. Sir John Kaye remarks:

> "But now the English themselves had placed in the hands of their enemies, not a fiction, but a fact of tremendous significance, to be turned against them as a deadly instrument of destruction."

The sepoys of the 19th Native Infantry at Berhampur and those of the 34th Native Infantry at Barrackpore knew about this. However, they decided to act only when asked to use them. They did not have to wait for long.

At the beginning of February 1857, the sepoys of the 19th Regiment were suspected of having risen over the use of new cartridges for practice, as it could offend their religious edicts, resulting in their social boycott, rendering them rootless in the community. Ultimately, the regiment was disarmed and disbanded. This was what had, in fact, occurred.

The 19th Native Regiment, stationed at Berhampur (in Odisha), on February 27, 1857, received information about the controversial greased cartridges from its detachment to Barrackpore. They were terrorised by the threat posed to their religion. As the sepoys gathered and discussed the explosive news, some noise broke out as they debated the topic heatedly.

Major Mitchell, the commanding officer, was terrorised by the noise and thought that his unit had risen. In undue haste, he summoned cannons and other military units garrisoned not far from there. His fears proved baseless as the sepoys had no plans to rise. However, a court of enquiry was constituted, which found the sepoys' act to be treason and ordered the regiment's disbandment. As the disbandment could be a cause of incitement to the native units located nearby, it was decided to march the sepoys to Barrackpore for this purpose. It hit the road on the 20th of March and reached the outskirts of Barrackpore on the 30th. It was here that Mitchell received alarming information that the 34th Regiment at Barrackpore had risen the previous day, under the leadership of Mangal Pande, and one officer had been cut down. Mitchell was now in a conundrum about where to proceed further.

Any book on the 1857 Uprising remains incomplete without the heroic single-handed revolution by Mangal Pande. Let us first tell the daring tale of sacrifice by this youthful sepoy, and then we shall turn our attention back to our mysterious protagonist, who was by now active in his secret movement.

9: The Maiden Sacrifice

Born in Ballia and recruited in the Bengal army in 1849, Mangal Pande was approximately 30 years old in 1857. He was posted in the 5th Company of the 34th Native Regiment, then garrisoned at Barrackpore, 32 kilometres from the then capital at Calcutta.

Perceiving resistance from the native sepoys, the use of new controversial cartridges was suspended. A few days later, however, the English officers once again behaved haughtily. They knew well that reintroducing the controversial cartridge could force the sepoys to revolt. Even the *Gazette*, issued from Calcutta, warned:

> "The Company Government has brought people under its influence, yet it never signifies that local people would approve of the alien government. They think we are foreigners, and we must realize this fact."

At this point, General Hearsey was the commander-in-chief at Barrackpore, headquarters of the presidency army. He, too, received information regarding the probability of the mutiny. He thought that it was easier said than rising in revolt. If they revolted, they would have neither shelter nor support, as they would not be able to endure the English power. Moreover, they would lose their jobs. So, the English officers paid little heed to such talks. On the other hand, he was being advised by his own officers that the drill with the cartridges should be suspended, because it would be next to impossible to restrain the sepoys if they chose to rise.

Hearsey disliked such remarks. He admitted that the new rifles had caused consternation among the ranks. Yet, he was not inclined to admit that the sepoys could commit anything as rumoured. In his view, the sepoys accepted the Company as their protector and preserver. His cocksure arrogance became all the more explicit when he said that Barrackpore was not Berhampur.

Saturday, March 29, 1857. History was being created that forenoon. The previous night, the sepoys had convened a meeting to discuss the fallout of the disputed cartridge and what was being done across the land to resist the English. They were told that May 31 had been fixed as the day of the Uprising. The Revolution Anthem was also sung (it is given in Appendix 'A' to this book). After the agenda, the sepoys sat in a relaxed mood; maybe *bhang* (hemp) was also consumed. Mangal Pande was excited, maybe he was intoxicated. He mistook it for the fact that he was supposed to rise the following morning.

For troops, the daily routine on Saturday was somewhat different from other weekdays. The morning PT (physical training) was not held, and the parade was brief. Officers and men were in a relaxed mood, wanting to catch some extra sleep or finish some sundry tasks. Of course, those on duty had to be on their posts. The sun shone brightly overhead as if intent on sending down additional energy. The place, not being very far from the sea, was quite hot and humid in the forenoon, disallowing the perspiration to dry up, and making them all restless.

Mangal Pande felt restless more than all others. He failed to understand why his comrades were so slack and calm. He was utterly confused, thinking it was the day of the uprising, yet no one seemed to act. And then his patience gave way. He picked up his musket, stuffed his pockets with cartridges, examined his sword, slipped it into the sheath, and walked to the quarter guard with long, resolute steps, calling his comrades to come along. At the same time, the sepoys on duty looked at him curiously.

Standing before the cannon, he roared, "Arrey! Why are you so quiet? It's the revolution day, isn't it? Rise if you are men and come along. Now don't hide yourself. Our religion is under threat."

He noticed a few sepoys walking up to him; this enthused him, and now his voice reverberated through the entire parade ground opposite the quarter guard, "Brothers, let us charge the enemy. Slaughter every Englishman here." When he saw the sepoys hesitating, he continued, "If you don't come, I'll fight the enemy all alone."

He thumped back and forth, trying to excite the comrades. All eager eyes were fixed on him, yet there was no movement from any quarter.

About this time, Lieutenant Baugh, the adjutant, was informed that some sepoys were in a state of excitement. Immediately, he armed himself, mounted his horse and galloped to the scene. The British Sergeant Major Hewson, too, had made it to the parade ground. When he saw that Mangal Pande was ordering the bugler to sound the assembly, he fired his pistol at him but missed. He then ordered Jemadar Ishwari Prasad to arrest Mangal Pande. The two were equal in rank, but the English considered themselves superior to the native sepoys and ordered them even if they possessed no such power. Ishwari Prasad little liked this order. He only said that none of his men were there, and that he alone would not be able to bring him under control. Furious at this reply, Hewson ordered Ishwari Prasad to arm himself and report to him.

At this point, Mangal Pande, being behind the station gun, was hidden from view, so Hewson warned Baugh not to go to the left, as he could be shot. Baugh asked him where the revolutionary was when Mangal Pande fired at the adjutant but missed the aim; the shot, however, hit the horse, and the two came down on the ground. Baugh hurriedly freed himself from the horse and took out the pistol. Meantime, Hewson attacked Mangal Pande, but he ducked and hit him back with the butt of his musket, bringing him down to the ground. Baugh was still on the ground, so Mangal Pande took out his sword and struck him on the shoulder. It was at this hour that the sepoys present there hit the two Englishmen.

Hearing the sound of firing, more sepoys ran to the ground, but they did not participate in the fray. One of them was Sheikh Paltu. The word 'paltu' signifies a person who goes back on his word. He backed out of the revolution. He stepped towards Mangal Pande, who was unaware of him, a native sepoy. Tall and sturdy, Paltu held Mangal Pande from behind. He tried to get free but could not. The other sepoys asked Paltu to release him, but to no avail. They even kicked him and hit him with pebbles, but Paltu did not buzz.

On the other hand, the captor shouted for help. When none came to his aid, he let go of Mangal Pande and ran to one side. By this time, the two fallen Englishmen had taken to their heels.

Describing this incident, Kaye has written in his book:

> "...Mungul Pandy, hidden by the station gun in front of the guard, took aim and fired at the Adjutant; but missing him, wounded his charger, and brought both horse and rider to the ground. Baugh then, disentangling himself, took one of his pistols from the holsters and fired at the Sepoy. The shot did not take effect, so he drew his sword and closed with the man, who also had drawn his tulwar, and then there was a sharp hand-to-hand conflict, in which the odds were against the Sepoy, for the sergeant-major came up and took part in the affray. But Mungul Pandy was a desperate man, and strokes of his tulwar fell heavily upon his assailants;

> and he might, perhaps, have dispatched them both, if a Mahomedan Sepoy, of the Grenadier Company, named Sheikh Paltoo, had not seized the mutineer and averted his blows."

He writes further:

> "Some of the Sepoys of the Guard struck the wounded officers on the ground with the butt-ends of their muskets, and one fired his piece at them; and when Sheikh Paltoo called upon them to arrest the mutineer, they abused him, and said if he did not release Mungul Pandy, they would shoot him. But he held the desperate fanatic until Baugh and the sergeant-major had escaped, and doubtless to his fidelity they owed their lives."

While all this was in progress, General Hearsey, who was in his house, was informed of the tumult in his regiment. His two sons had recently donned the military uniform as officers. He got ready and moved to the quarter guard with his sons. He straightened his pistol and commanded the sepoys posted there to imprison Mangal Pande. He warned that he would shoot anyone not following his order. Seeing a high officer among them, the sepoys were now alert. They were about to get ready to catch the revolutionary.

By this time, Mangal Pande was tired. His comrades had not given him direct support. When he saw that they were about to abide by Hearsey's bidding, he put the muzzle of his musket to his neck and pressed the trigger with his foot. As the sound of fire rent the air, he fell bleeding with his uniform ablaze. He was destined to live for a few more days.

Mangal Pande was treated for his wound, limited to stopping bleeding merely, as the English knew well what punishment he was to be meted out. On April 6, the court-martial interrogated him about the influences on him, but he took all the guilt upon himself. He was sentenced to death by hanging. April 18 was set as the sentencing date. In the intervening period, the 19th Native Regiment, from Berhampur, was disbanded on March 31.

It was April 8, 1857, ten full days from the date of punishment. It was early in the morning. Mangal Pande sat up in his dingy cell as pain disturbed him from sleep. The wound in the neck was still far from recovery. Maybe he thought what would cause more pain: stretching the neck or the pressure of the rope on the wound. Ishwari Prasad was incarcerated in the adjoining cell. He was charged with ordering his sepoys not to arrest Mangal Pande. Though small, he had played a role in the tiny uprising against the foreign masters; he, too, was sentenced to death, to be executed on April 21.

It was amazing that an English officer came knocking, accompanied by sepoys, to take Mangal Pande with him. A smile emerged on the prisoner's face. A few moments later, he was walking to the gallows under the sharp pointed bayonets, when he looked towards Ishwari Prasad's cell. He did not expect him to be awake at that early hour, but he found him standing, looking out. Mangal Pande tried to say something to him, but the bayonet pinched him on the back, forcing him to keep walking. Ten days ahead of the appointed date, he was hanged in the presence of all troops. His physique was destroyed for sure, yet the soul and the ideas never die; his sacrifice proved just this. It was the first sacrifice of the 1857 Uprising. Now the land was bracing herself to prepare thousands of such bravehearts who would sacrifice themselves to free her from the imperialist shackles.

As we tell the inspiring tale of the immortal Mangal Pande, people like Sheikh Paltu do not deserve a mention, yet we might. Due to his vicious role in the uprising, he was promoted to the rank of havildar; however, a few days later, he was murdered in the military lines. The entire 34th Native Regiment was not considered trustworthy, so the court of enquiry recommended disbanding it as well. Kaye reveals this decision in his book:

> "The men [sepoys] still went about with their arms in their hands, and there was scarcely a European in Barrackpore who believed that he was safe from the violence."

As a consequence of the apprehension, all sepoys present in the station were disarmed and sent off to their hometowns. However, there are doubts about whether they all returned to their families. It is widely believed that many of them headed to other units and contacted other sepoys. This spread disaffection in the entire army. The sepoys were already dissatisfied owing to the English economic policies and prejudice against native sepoys in the army. The previous year, that is, in 1856, Awadh had been subjugated by the English illegally on a false pretext. This too had caused them hurt as a large number of sepoys in the Bengal Army came from Awadh and the surrounding areas. The coercion to use the greased cartridge was like adding salt to the injury. They were now faced with a conundrum.

As disaffection across the northern part of the land mounted, many other rumours floated in the air too; they were spread by the wandering saints and messengers. Among others, one was this. The Crimean War took place from October 1853 to February 1856, fought chiefly between England and Russia, among other powers. England had emerged victorious in it, yet a rumour went around in India that it had suffered a large number of casualties, resulting in numerous widows. The English government was undecided about what to do with these women and was actively considering sending them to India to arrange marriages with princes in different princely states. The offspring from such alliances would be Christian, which would give a fillip to their faith in the country. It was a mere rumour, but it could have a severe, adverse impact.

There was no end to such rumours, one such being about bone powder in wheat flour, as delineated in the *Meerut Gazetteer*:

> ". .. .it is certain, however, that in the early part of 1857 there were disquieting rumours afloat in the bazars of Meerut and among the native troops, especially those regarding the use of polluting grease in the preparation of the new cartridges about to be issued to the troops and the mixture of ground bones in the flour sold in the bazar, by which it was said that Government intended to destroy caste and religion of the people."

Kaye writes in his book about these rumours:

> "Now the disturbing rumour, cunningly circulated, took many portentous shapes. It was said that the officers of the British Government under the command from the Company and the Queen, had mixed ground bones with the flour and the salt sold in the Bazaars; that they had adulterated all the ghi [oil] with animal fat; that bones had been burnt with the common sugar of the country; and that not only bone-dust flour but the flesh of cows and pigs had been thrown into the wells to pollute the drinking water of the people."

How potent these rumours were can be gauged from the fact that the 'Meerut flour' had earned such an ill repute that in Kanpur, no person, sepoy or civilian, would touch it despite it being cheaper than other supplies in the market.

What started from Barrackpore spread to the cantonments across India, and the sepoys communicated it to civilians. How efficient this communication system was can be understood by the following extract from John Kaye's book:

> "The news of the first outbreak and massacre at Kabul, in 1841, and also of the subsequent destruction of the British Army in the Pass, reached Calcutta through the bazaars of Mirath [Meerut] and Karnal some days before they found their way to the Government House from any official quarter; and the mutiny at Barrackpore was known by the Sipahis of the British force proceeding to Burmah [now Myanmar] before it reached the military and political chiefs by special express."

Two kinds of people specifically contributed to spreading this information. The first ones were the messengers assigned to deliver mail between district headquarters and cantonments. Each military unit eagerly awaited these messengers, who were like modern-day dispatch riders, and they continue to be eagerly awaited, especially in units where the use of mobile phones is barred. These messengers also worked as a link between the sepoys and their families. As soon as a messenger arrived in a military unit, the sepoys would surround him and enquire whether there were any letters for them; they also took this opportunity to learn what was happening across the country and the world. These messengers did not come daily. For instance, the one from Delhi to Meerut rode a cart twice a week. Often, he also brought sundry items on demand from Delhi, which added to his income, so they grew quite close to one another.

The other kind that contributed to spreading information included saints, *faqirs* (alms-seekers) and *madaris* (street magicians and jugglers). It was no difficult task for this segment of wanderers to come into contact with people who too readily trusted them. The protagonist of this book is also a Sanyasi, described by contemporary writers as a Hindu faqir, who played a vital role in inciting the revolution while residing at Kali Paltan Temple in Meerut. The cause of elation is that this face, which was yet wrapped in mystery, has come to light through my profound research. He is the person who went on to become one of India's all-time great personalities. We are just about to reveal who this harbinger of the Uprising was and how he accomplished it.

10: Spreading Disaffection

Perceiving the changing demeanour of the sepoys, the Sanyasi could easily guess that his words were making a due impact. He believed that only the final strike was needed. As he was given the date of May 31 for the Uprising, he was eagerly waiting for the day. The sepoys, on their part, too opined that they would act only when their training started. He had secured their silent assent that they would punish any traitor.

It was around this time that news filtered that the company officers were planning to commence training in the new cartridge at Meerut, too. The iron was growing hotter; a little more wait would make it red hot, when it would be ready to strike the final blow. Finding his goal close at hand, the Sanyasi had been working for an extended time, reducing his sleep to only a few hours. He was also formulating his final plan, keeping the local conditions in mind. Now he was actively keeping in touch with the sepoys and civilians, while keeping his eyes and ears open. It was when the first opportunity struck.

It was the 13th of April in the year 1857; each year, the festival of Baisakhi was, and is, celebrated on this day, as it is a major farming-based festival of the Punjab; all farmers, whether Hindu or Muslim, joined in. The sepoys coming from the Punjab those days were mostly Muslims, but they joined the celebration. As they all sat down to their meals, one sepoy, Brijmohan Singh, revealed that he had torn the disputed envelope with his teeth. They were all shocked by this revelation. They felt downtrodden when he said that all sepoys would have to use them sooner or later.

The other sepoys appeared tranquil, but a tempest was rising within them. The same night, Brijmohan's house was set on fire. These fires became routine, with those whose activities were questionable. Some of these fires broke out in English households as well. One such occurred in the quartermaster stores. The local historian Amit Pathak has also described this incident. It is mentioned in the *Meerut Gazetteer* in these words:

> "A trooper, by name Brijmohan, announced to his comrades that he had used them [disputed cartridges], and that all would have to do so. The result was that Brijmohan's house was set on fire on the 13th of April, and from this date incendiary fires became frequent."

The English guessed that these fires occurred due to excessive heat and loo, a hot wind that blows in this region at this time of the year, when such fires were routine in view of the fact that the roofs of most buildings were made from dry grass and wooden structures, which caught fire rather easily.

Ten days later, all sepoys took their sacred books in their hands and vowed that they would not use the cartridge when given to them for practice. The embers were being stoked now, and mild flames could be seen rising in them.

As April approached its close, the Sanyasi was satisfied that a favourable atmosphere was gradually coming into being, in which the narrative surrounding the controversial cartridge was playing a prominent part. On April 26, two days after the sepoys at Meerut refused to use the cartridge, in Ambala, the native sepoys rose against the forcible use of the new cartridge. The insurrection continued for five days, during which they set the English bungalows, armoury and stable on fire. The ruthlessness with which this outbreak was crushed is evident in the corpses recently recovered from the wells.

The news from Barrackpore had reached Meerut, too. The common points of discussion among sepoys were centred around the outbreaks occurring at different places and the unjust conduct of the British in Awadh. Meanwhile, the 7th Native Regiment, at Lucknow, had been disarmed and disbanded over the same issue. The Sanyasi happily received the information concerning firings, showing how excited the sepoys were. The letters from their families also pressurised them not to use the contentious cartridge, as it would destroy their caste and religion. The sepoys were visiting and corresponding with other sepoys posted elsewhere, expressing their anguish.

Rumours had become the order of the day. While the sepoys rose in different places, the English remained arrogant as usual. They thought that the sepoys had no way out but to serve them. This mental inclination was going to cost them dearly in the coming days.

11: Failed Attempt at Rising

April 24, 1857. Refusing to learn from the blunders committed elsewhere, the English determined to use the new cartridge at Meerut as well. The sepoys had come to know of this decision the previous evening, and that the 3rd Cavalry Regiment would be the first to be forced to use it. After the evening roll call, the sepoys gathered at one place. They took a vow with the sacred Ganga water and holy texts in their palms. They were all tense, unable to sleep all night. Some of them went to the Sanyasi for some pacification. However, he told them what the brave were supposed to do in such a drastic situation. He emphatically said that silently bearing atrocity only increases it.

The 3rd Cavalry Regiment fell in on the parade ground and formed in contingents, each comprising 90 cavalrymen. After the initial routine, Colonel Carmichael Smyth ordered the distribution of the disputed cartridges to one of these contingents. It is said these were dummy cartridges used for training. It appears that they were issued in order to affirm the sepoys' willingness or unwillingness to bite them with teeth. Of the 90 sepoys, 85 refused to accept or use them. They said they were not revolting but were devoted to their faiths; they could not do anything that would prove a blot on their community life. Smyth adamantly pressured them, and when his threats bore no fruit, he ordered these 85 sepoys to be thrown in jail and a court-martial be held against them.

Unlike other regiments where the sepoys had risen, this regiment or contingent was not disarmed or disbanded; rather, it was decided to court-martial 85 of them for disobedience, which ultimately took place on the 6th, 7th, and 8th of May. In just three days, the case was decided, and the sentence was pronounced. This eager haste explains what kind of justice was meted out to them.

The havildar of this platoon was Matadin. It was he who protested against the distribution of the greased cartridge. He clearly said that he and his comrades believed that the way they were being asked to use the cartridges, there was enough space to doubt the intention; moreover, the sepoys were not being taken into confidence. On their part, the English officers were not inclined to allay their suspicion. They could have had the cartridges examined by specialists, and the sepoys could have been taken to the place of manufacturing, as Meerut was one of the places where the cartridges were being packed. These steps could have convinced the sepoys that their faiths were not under any threat. On the contrary, the English had grown steadfastly arrogant. They seemed to be bent upon crushing the Indians' pride somehow.

The *Meerut Gazetteer* notes that this court-martial also comprised 9 Hindu and 6 Muslim officials, of whom 10 belonged to Meerut and 5 to Delhi. However, the fact that has been cunningly concealed is that all senior officials were English. Hierarchy is the most important factor in the army; that is, the contention of several junior officers can be negated by one single superior officer. This text also writes that the prisoners said nothing in defence. How could this be possible? They were for sure denied any opportunity to speak. It also writes that of 15 native officials, 14 considered them guilty; it simply overlooks the presence of English officers. Even Kaye admits this discrepancy when he writes:

> "Some Native officials from the Delhi regiments had been sitting on the great Meerut Court Martial; but how far they sympathised with the prisoners cannot be confidently declared."

On May 8, the court martial sentenced all 85 native troops to ten years' rigorous imprisonment, after which the court was dismissed. When this judgement was dispatched to the commanding officer of the 3rd Regiment, he reduced the sentence of 11 sepoys to five years, saying that they were under the age of 18 years. This sequence of events also reveals how they could violate the laws and rules made by them with impunity, and serious questions can be raised about their judicial procedure.

We are aware of the names of these 85 sepoys. Their names are carved in the memorial located in Victoria Park, where the new jail was located. These names can also be read at the First War of Freedom Memorial in the Meerut Museum premises, which has been built to commemorate the great Uprising. We have appended this list to this book, which begins with the name of Matadin. It contains the names of both Hindus and Muslims; most of the former ones belonged to the Awadh region, while most of the latter ones came from the region of the Punjab, which now forms part of the state of Haryana.

May 9, 1857

The way the English had insulted the native sepoys showed that they were not yet satisfied. They overlooked that their act had already violated the Indians' limit of tolerance and could lead to an explosive consequence. Acting arrogantly, the English did something they could have done without. They thought that they would be able to terrorise and scare the remaining native sepoys into submission, but this was not what ultimately happened.

The 85 sepoys had been sentenced, yet there were several Englishmen who favoured a still harsher sentence, so that no more of them could ever dare to disobey them. To pronounce the sentence openly, all military regiments at Meerut, including the magazine, were ordered to fall in the main parade ground. The regiments were positioned such that all native sepoys were in direct range of the cannons. All European infantrymen and cavalrymen were armed and ready. Two high-powered guns were also brought in. Even the native sepoys working in the magazine were ordered to stand alongside other sepoys. Thus, the English had arranged the men such that any 'undesirable' act on the part of the native sepoys could be crushed instantaneously. In contrast, the native sepoys had their muskets but no ammunition. Tension could be clearly perceived on all faces, native or foreign.

It was quite hot while some clouds kept playing with the sun. In this monsoon month, humidity was at its peak, leading to heavy sweating and discomfort. When the sun hid behind the clouds, some respite could be felt, but this proved transitory each time. When the sun shone in all its glory, the helpless eyes would look for some shade. These eyes were helpless not merely for this reason, but also for the fact that a vicious game of barbarity and humiliation was being played before them. Yet, they were unable to do anything about it. Any protest at such a time could prove catastrophic to their very existence. They needed to live on to have achieved the revolution's goal. The worrisome situation before them was that they were ready for the revolution. However, they had been assigned May 31 for the purpose, which was still three weeks away. The situation was highly drastic.

The English were assured of their strength. They little hoped for an insurrection at Meerut, as the balance of power in Meerut favoured them, as against other cantonments across the country.

When all was set, the 85 sentenced sepoys were marched in. They were lined up in the middle, where they were visible to all troops, black or white. They were still in their military uniforms, together with their ranks and badges, but without arms. After this, the garrison commander read out their 'crime' and sentence, followed by the cashiering procedure; under it, their belts, ranks and badges were to be torn out. The English, with an intention to insult, not only pulled out their belts, ranks and badges, but also tore off their dresses together with socks and shoes.

In the book *The Mutiny of the Bengal Army*, the writer, who identifies himself as 'By one who has served under Sir Charles Napier', writes:

> "At daybreak on that morning [May 9], all the troops in the station, leaving the guards standing, paraded on the 60th Rifle parade ground; the Carabineers, the 60th Rifles, the 3rd Light Cavalry, the 11th and 20th Regiments of Native Infantry, a light field battery, and a troop of horse artillery. The Carabineers and the Rifles were then ordered to load and be ready, and the Horse Artillery the same. This done, the mutineers were marched on to the ground; the European troops and Artillery guns being so placed that the least movement of disaffection or insurrection would have been followed by instant slaughter."

Then the ironmen were summoned to rivet iron bars around their necks, waist and arms. It is believed they were also given physical punishment. The sepoys begged for mercy and sympathy, but no heed was paid to what they had to say. Kaye describes their plight and how loyalty had been repaid with atrocity:

> "It was a piteous spectacle, and many there were moved with great compassion when they saw the despairing gesture of those wretched men, among whom were some of the very

> flower of the regiment—soldiers who had served the British Government in trying circumstances and in strange places, and who had never wavered in their allegiance. Lifting up their hands and lifting up their voices, the prisoners implored the General to have mercy upon them, and not to consign them to so ignominious a doom. Then, seeing there was no hope, they turned to their comrades and reproached them for quietly suffering this disgrace to descend upon them."

However, the sepoys could not come to their rescue in the face of 'loaded field-guns and those grooved rifles, and the glittering sabres of the Dragoons'. This is what happens when ominous signs are about to eclipse all good things. Something of the sort was bound to occur with the English.

The entire procedure lasted close to two hours. After this, the punished sepoys were marched away to the new jail, located about three kilometres away. The officials wanted to unleash a wave of terror among the civilians, too, so the contingent was taken through the nearby market instead of taking the Mall Road, which was a straight route. At this time, they were under the guard of native sepoys. Finding no other English officer with them, the incarcerated sepoys used foul words for their comrades; they termed them cowards; they said that they were defiling their castes and religions. In the market, some civilians had lined up to see what was unfolding before their eyes. They too cursed the guards and asked them what they got in return for their docile servitude to the English. This was making all native sepoys restless and fretful. One guard went to the extent of raising his musket against a civilian.

Listening to what was happening in the market, the *tawaifs* (dancing girls) also arrived and took up a vantage point. It was quite usual for the sepoys to visit their *kothas* (places for live performance) for entertainment. Today, these very women swore at them and termed them devoid of masculinity and vigour. They did not stop at that; they removed their glass bangles and threw them at their faces – an act of expressing extreme disapproval. The guards kept their cool somehow. The swords in their sheaths were growing restless, but they knew that rising at that time could lead to utter failure. At this time, the English were fully ready and could crush them in minutes. The sepoys were trained to win; how could they play a game of sure defeat? The guards looked at the Sanyasi who stood at the kerb looking at them meaningfully.

In the review after the outbreak, the English have considered marching the punished sepoys to jail under the guard of other native sepoys a grave mistake. Governor General Lord Canning wrote that the way they were taken to the jail corrupted the guard sepoys' minds, as the punished sepoys cursed them, and this finally led to the rebellion. Read what he wrote to Vernon Smith on June 5, 1857:

> "The riveting of the men's fetters on parade, occupying as it did, several hours, in the presence of many who were already ill-disposed, and many who believed in the cartridge fable, must have struck the brigade to the quick. The consigning the eighty- five prisoners, after such a ceremony, to the gaol, with no other than a native guard over them, was, considering the nature of their offence, and the known temper of the part of the Army, a folly that is inconceivable."

***

By that afternoon, having secured the prisoners in the new jail, the sepoys returned to their barracks. A Saturday had no afternoon PT session, so the sepoys used this time to enjoy themselves, visit the market or another place, or play games. However, they had no such plan on this day, as the English had completely vitiated the atmosphere.

They were all restless; their innate grief found unexpected expression. The insult they were subjected to this morning seemed unbearable. The junior sepoys wanted to take immediate revenge, but the seniors were somehow restraining them, advising them to wait until the right time.

A young sepoy blurted out madly, "When will that right time come?"

He was informed that they would have to wait until May 31, when the entire country would rise together, and in one sweep, all the English would be driven out. Their sentiments were manifest in their conduct. Lunchtime was often a noisy affair as they talked and joked. It was also the time to plan for the evening hangout. The atmosphere was quite different that day. There was hardly any talking among them.

"We are serving them, does that mean we have no self-respect?" a young sepoy said.

"How can we see our faith being defiled?" another sepoy almost screamed.

"Keep silent!" said a senior sepoy. "Don't let this anger subside. If you speak out, it will evaporate."

Once again, the mess was enveloped in a pin-drop silence. There was much humidity in the atmosphere, leading to extreme heat. The sepoys returned to their barracks. Made from earthen plates and dry grass, the barracks were located quite near the mess. One hut housed three sepoys, while havildars and above were allotted a separate hut. They had to share common baths. In comparison, the English troops were housed in brick-and-mortar barracks with all facilities, including recreational facilities. So far as the English officers were concerned, they were allotted spacious bungalows with all facilities which could be imagined in those days.

Sadar Bazar was hardly a distance away, just 500 metres. As the sepoys were tackling their anxiety mixed with anger, they avoided visiting the market, which was their favourite joint, especially during the weekend. Only a few went. In the market, they were highly respected, as they provided income for traders. They could also get commodities on credit. Today, they felt that the traders were not treating them well or were just ignoring them.

Of those who went, they found that the traders were unusually unwilling to sell them goods on credit. It is said that since the Chapati and Lotus campaigns came into existence, traders had stopped giving credit to sepoys. When they protested, arguments ensued. The traders believed that the revolution had commenced elsewhere, but as the means of communication and transport were all under the English, they were not allowing the news to leak out. It was also rumoured that in Sotiganj, a native sepoy had thrashed a European, but this was not confirmed. Rumours were playing their part. The occurrence in the morning seemed to have changed everything forever.

Towards the evening, dark clouds covered the sky, making the day look even clumsier. The Sanyasi had set his seat in the open as his sermon time approached. Soon, the sepoys arrived and sat in the grass; they felt that a visit to the temple could provide them with succour. The Sanyasi, however, was there to make the most of the opportunity that had come across. Reciting a Vedic verse, he soon came to his favourite topic, and today's occurrence had invigorated him completely. He said in his usual eloquence, "There can be no greater insult than this."

"We will have to bear with this insult for a few more days," said a sepoy.

"Why do you wish to bear with it any more?" the Sanyasi pointed out.

"You know that we need to rise on May 31."

"Maybe, but are you ready to live with this disrespect for three more weeks? Your silence would only encourage the English to insult you even more bitterly," the Sanyasi retorted in a harsher tone, making the sepoys sink in deep thought, when he added, "May 31 is a Sunday, so is tomorrow."

The Sanyasi warned that if their plan was somehow divulged to the English, they would disarm them. How then would they be able to rise? It was a powerful argument, forcing the sepoys to think more deeply, yet they could not reach the level of consciousness that would compel them to revolt instantly. The Sanyasi did his best to excite the sepoys to rise just then or the following morning. He also told them what they were expected to do in the insurrection.

The sepoys were angry, no doubt, yet their intensity was not high enough to trigger an outbreak. After his sermon and evening prayers, when the Sanyasi distributed Prasad among the sepoys, he appeared to be in a trance. Disappointment deepened the slender lines on his forehead as he felt that his plan had failed miserably. He felt that the mental excitement created by that day's proceedings could not be sustained until the end of the month, so he wanted the Uprising to start immediately, even if in an unplanned manner.

The sepoys returned and crowded into the mess for meals. Just about then, it started to rain amid thundering clouds. Humidity ebbed away as freshness enveloped. Soon, they were all in their barracks arranging their beds. Lying on them, it is difficult to say if they were awake or asleep.

***

A moot question is: Was the 31st of May set as the date for the insurrection? If yes, who fixed it? There is no direct evidence on this, yet there is no dearth of circumstantial evidence. With the massive scale at which the Uprising erupted, we are inclined to conjecture that there was some plan for sure. It is likely that Nana Saheb Peshwa and his advisor, Azimulla Khan, visited Meerut in March or April of that year to assess the situation when they were in Delhi to meet the Mughal ruler. Kaye expresses amazement that a man like Nana Saheb, who seldom travelled beyond Bithur, had become hyperactive. He writes:

> "Nana Sahib of Bhitur [Bithur], the adopted son of the Peshwa, Baji Rao. He was not given to distant journeyings; indeed, he was seldom seen beyond the limits of his own estate. But in the early months of 1857, having visited Kalpi, he made a journey to Delhi, and a little later in the year, paid a visit to Lakhnao."

Much was at stake for Nana Saheb, so it is very likely that he was instrumental in setting May 31 as the date of the Uprising. It was on May 30 that the sepoys in Kanpur finally rose in revolt, which also points to some preplan about the date. There was, for sure, a given date, as several revolutionaries had met in the forest in Mathura, where Nana Saheb was also present. He had pinned his hopes on Meerut, confident of the extensive work being undertaken there, and is said to have visited it too. Colonel Keith Young, later the Judge Advocate General, in a letter to his wife, published in the book form titled *1857-Delhi*, edited by his wife and others, writes:

> "That Nana was the man who used to drive up and down the Mall at Meerut, when we were there, with a European coachman."

Later, Keith Young negated his own assertion. Our protagonist, Sanyasi, was in Meerut as part of this plan too. We are about to reveal his identity soon. A pertinent question is: Why did the Sanyasi want the Uprising to start immediately, before the planned date? He probably felt that the sepoys were at their highest level of excitement, and such a state could not be sustained every day. A three-week recess could simmer down this excitement, leaving nothing to happen on the given date.

It was also quite possible that the plan could leak out in the meantime, which would warn the English who would ensure that the Uprising did not erupt at all, while at present they appeared drowned in overconfidence and complacency. An unplanned insurrection would be better than no outbreak. His logic went that, when the sepoys were not ready to rise on the day of the sentence, it was very unlikely that they would rise on the given date too.

The iron was hot enough, only it had to be brought to a state where the hammer could be struck hard against it. He could not afford to see his plan fail without making an earnest endeavour. After the sepoys left, he sat down, thinking about how he could use this opportunity, how he could force the sepoys to rise in an armed struggle against the imperialist masters.

Soon, a concrete plan began to take shape in his mind, and as he thought over its pros and cons, he felt satisfied. The well-known smile now became manifest on his lips. It was raining. He spread a sheet on the ground near the Aughardani and lay down. The shower sprinkled over him in a soft, delicate touch, sending him into the embrace of sleep. In no time, he was dreaming about how the Uprising would take place.

12: The Volcanic Eruption

Sunday, May 10, 1857. A lazy day like any other holiday in an army unit. Today was destined to see the great Uprising, but for now, the air was without a trace of it; maybe it was all a camouflaged affair. Amit Pathak writes in his book, *Living History*, that many servants working in British households did not report for work. He has also stated that some sepoys may have gone to Delhi the previous night to inform their comrades about the action they were going to take. It is also speculated that some servants warned the English of the incoming storm, yet they remained confident in their might.

The sepoys were not up to anything by now. Some of them were playing together while others thought it better to catch up on sleep. When the breakfast bell rang, some of them ignored it, wanting more sleep than calories. It had rained the previous night, so the weather was pleasant. The previous day's tension seemed to have been wiped out by the night's rest. Hardly anyone had visited the market the day before, but some of them needed to buy things, so they decided to go to Sadar Bazar after lunch. Its retail market was a long, straight street with Bombay Bazar at one end and Police Street on the other. The alleys on one side of the market opened in the wholesale market, while those on the other led to Bankers Street and residential houses. Thus, it had multiple entry points.

The sepoys entered the alley from near the police station on Bankers Street, where it was located then. They noticed that near the main gate, two peons of the cantonment office, uniformed and armed with swords, were looking at the sepoys with a meaningful gaze. The sepoys felt something extraordinary about them, yet were unable to perceive anything; they kept walking towards the market. The previous day, the few sepoys who visited it had not been treated well by traders, so they wanted to just finish buying before heading back to their regiments.

Sadar Bazar was established in 1806; both its retail and wholesale sections continue to exist to date and are normally crowded due to the large number of shops, attracting many buyers. Those days, it was quite sparse. Since it was a Sunday, there were more people than usual; some came just to hang out. The previous day's anxiety did not seem to be present, or maybe the traders wanted to focus on their business. In addition to sepoys and civilians, a sizeable number of European men and women were buying their necessities. Suddenly, a rumour spread, leaving the entire area tense. The *Meerut Gazetteer* notes about this rumour thus:

> "Between 5 and 6 pm, the cry that the Europeans were coming to take possession of the magazines of the Native Infantry spread through the Sadar Bazar and the lines of the 20th Native Infantry."

It was about five in the evening. Everything appeared as normal as normal could be. Just then, some noise rose from near one end, and shopkeepers began moving their goods into their shops and shutting their doors. A trader picked up a staff and struck an Englishman. As he fell, he approached the others in the same threatening manner. And then the shops started hurriedly shutting their wooden doors. In no time, numerous people appeared in the street with sticks, javelins, axes, swords and knives, and began attacking the Europeans, as if under a plan. The entire market reverberated with commotion, screams and slogans.

It was about this time that the policemen rushed in from the police station and started to attack the Englishmen they came across. The Europeans were all too confused by this sudden change of atmosphere and scurried across to find secure shelter. The policemen were leading the civilians armed with domestic weapons; they were at the same time shouting not to allow any *Firangi* (foreigner) to escape alive.

In no time, the peaceful market had turned into a hub of indiscriminate violence. According to unconfirmed sources, violence in the market began somewhat in this manner. The sepoys noticed that the Sanyasi, who lived in the Kali Paltan Temple, entered the market from one end. One by one, he stopped at several shops briefly, and talked to the traders almost thus:

Sanyasi: Lala, are you aware of what is going to happen today?
Trader: What do you think will happen today?

Sanyasi: You all are going to die today. All sepoys too will die. The English are coming. They will take possession of the weapons of all Indians.

Before the trader could ask him something, the Sanyasi moved on to the next shop and conducted a brief conversation on almost the same lines.

The violence that started in the Sadar Bazar spread through the entire town. People were looking for any English signs and symbols to destroy. The way violence spread, it appeared that all this had been preplanned. Kaye writes in his book:

> "... the report gained strength that the English soldiery, armed to the teeth, would soon be let loose amongst them; that every Sepoy before nightfall would have fetters on his wrists; that the People would be given up to massacre, and the Bazaars to plunder."

The *Meerut Gazetteer* writes:

> "The bad characters of the city and bazar were assembled before a shot had been fired, and armed with clubs, spears and swords and any other weapon that they could lay hands upon, collected in crowds in every lane and alley and at every outlet of the bazars, while the residents of the wretched hamlets which had been allowed to spring up all round the bazar and between it and the city were to be seen similarly armed, pouring out to share in the plunder which they knew would soon commence."

Violence spread through the Sadar Bazar and the surrounding areas. A large number of Europeans had fallen victim to it. Several buildings were engulfed in fire. All scholars agree that the violence initially erupted in Sadar Bazar, and the way it started suggests the possibility of a plan in existence, because not only local residents but also a large number of people from nearby villages joined the Uprising. This is also evidenced by the fact that several shopkeepers had stopped selling goods on credit to Europeans. It is believed that the Sanyasi often visited this market, and he had predicted that the English rule would come to an end upon the completion of 100 years in 1857.

Major G.W. Williams has, in his report '*Narrative of Events*' said that he found the entire area to the south of the nullah and Begum Bridge empty, as it had witnessed the storm which shook India, and the destruction visible here was caused not by the troops on the might of their arms and discipline, but by an uncontrolled crowd, and this had happened when a large European military power was present here.

The English have attempted to undermine this Uprising in several ways. They have described it as a mere sepoys' revolt, overlooking the participation of the masses; however, the above report is a potent piece of evidence that shows civilians initiated the Uprising. Of course, now the sepoys were going to play a major role in it.

Obviously, when the Sanyasi perceived that the sepoys were unwilling to rise, he planned so that they would be forced to rise ultimately. So, he activated his contacts in the nearby villages, gathered armed people in the market, incited the civilians, and started violence when some sepoys were present there. He knew if the sepoys rose, all else would happen that could be desirable in the Uprising. His efforts had materialised into erupting the volcano; now he needed to guide it in the proper direction, so he too rushed back to the temple.

13: The Sepoys Ultimately Rise

When the civilians started action against the Europeans in Sadar Bazar, there were also a few sepoys present there. They, too, heard that the English were about to disarm them. They had seen the Sanyasi busily moving in the market with a resolute face. A soldier's first love is his weapon. The time for action had ultimately arrived. With the rising commotion, they hurried back to their barracks, many of them on the double. Their demeanour was no more wavering; their eyes divulged a firm resolve. Surendra Nath Sen writes in his book *Eighteen Fifty-seven*:

> "Caught unawares, the sepoys were panic-stricken. Still in undress and without arms, they hurried back to their lines, not knowing what to do. As happens in such a crisis, the instinct of self-preservation asserted itself."

As they reached their units, they called their comrades and informed them that the time for rising was right there and that the English were on the way to disarm them. Even the Sanyasi had hinted at this the previous night. In minutes, the sepoys had all gathered, first heading to the armoury. When the guard heard them, he allowed them to draw arms; no records were kept. They filled their pockets with as many cartridges as they wanted. A slogan went up to the sky, and then it rang with repeated calls – *Har-har Mahadev* and *Allah-o-Akbar*. Many a sepoy donned his uniform as it felt quite natural to him; however, he had not forgotten to remove the badges. Praising the native troops for their courage, Henry Mead has, in his book *The Sepoy Revolt*, written:

> "They were scarcely a match, numerically speaking, for

> the European troops, and had never been taught that against odds of two to one the Gora Logue had failed to be victorious. There were in the station two troops of European horse artillery, together with a field battery, whilst they were wholly destitute of guns. The dragoons could have fairly ridden down a couple of native cavalry regiments, and the 60th Rifles were at least a match for 2000 Sepoys. With such a prospect of speedy annihilation before them, they rose at six o'clock on Sunday afternoon, and set the first example of rebellion and murder."

Quite near the Kali Paltan Temple, a similar spectacle was unfolding in the 20th Infantry Regiment. You can find the Race Course here today. The sepoys were all collected in the ground near the mess, and they planned to march out under the command of the senior sepoys. They had hardly approached the gate when their commanding officer, Colonel John Finis, arrived mounted on his horse. He was informed of something unusual in his regiment. It is said that he was an influential and capable officer. He ordered the sepoys to halt and asked what they were up to. Bred with discipline, they stood rooted where they were. They now looked to each other about what they ought to do.

Just about then, the sepoys of the 3rd Native Cavalry entered the gate, mounted on their horses. Colonel Finis ordered them to be quiet, but they were in high excitement. Finding the commanding officer surrounded by native sepoys, some more European horsemen arrived on the scene. One of them shouted at the top of his voice: "Get back to your barracks. What are you doing here? Have you gone mad?"

The sentence had hardly been completed when a gunshot was fired, possibly by a sepoy of the 3rd Regiment. With its sound, the colonel fell off his horse, dead. The European troops had barely straightened their weapons when more gunshots were fired, and two more of them fell off their horses. The others tried to flee, but their fate was no different.

With this, all native sepoys had joined the Uprising; not only this, they had scored their first hit too. The sepoys then headed towards the cantonment area to the north of the nullah. A few of them saw Charles Dowson's bungalow (where the Ram Canteen is today). He was a senior veterinarian. The sepoys speculated that he was in the bungalow with his wife, as he was probably suffering from chickenpox, so he would not have gone to the church that Sunday evening.

As the sepoys entered the gate, they spotted Dowson standing in the verandah with a pistol in his hand. He had possibly heard the gunshots, so he was alert. As he saw the sloganeering sepoys, he understood what the matter was, and he fired his first shot; and that was all he could do. The sepoys acted quickly, throwing their *mashals* (fire-torches) on the roof made from dry grass. In minutes, the entire bungalow was rising in flames. Dowson ran into the bungalow. Probably, both husband and wife died burning, but their corpses were never recovered. This fact is mentioned in the records of the St John's Cemetery.

It is said that until this point, the sepoys of the 11th Infantry Regiment had been unwilling to rise; however, when the jubilant revolutionary sepoys passed by their unit and found that Colonel Finis and Dowson had died, they too were ready in minutes to expand the scope of the Uprising.

Being horse-mounted, it was rather convenient and quick for the sepoys of the 3rd Cavalry to go from one place to another. They moved quickly, destroying the English, their bungalows and symbols. They spread over the entire area of the large cantonment. At that time, the outer boundary of the Meerut cantonment was about 8 kilometres long, which sufficiently suggests its large size. Today, it has expanded over a much larger area.

Europe is a cold region, while India experiences extreme weather; in May, it experiences a very hot season. This was the reason the prayer time at St. John's Church, located in the northern part, was set late in the afternoon.

This church was established in 1819, quite near St. John's Cemetery. This formed part of the facilities that the Europeans had created for themselves in this part. As the sun rode to the west, the temperature ebbed gradually. With this, the European officers and their families were preparing to visit the church. Many of them had already descended the Mall Road to take the road to it. Just then, the sound of horse hooves was heard, and then one gunshot was heard from the direction of the Mall Road, followed by the second, the third and then many more. As a result, the entire area was filled with screams and shouts. Everyone started running hither and thither to save his life. The native sepoys were quickly taking possession of the area. They attacked only men, but allowed women and children to go away. Only one woman was killed, who had held a horse's reins; she was crushed under the horse's feet.

The sepoys specifically aimed for bungalows and offices, all of which were set on fire. Wherever they found wires, they snapped them. They wanted to erase all English signs and symbols. What an amazing sight it was to see the Europeans taking to their heels in fright, despite having the magazine under their control. They had deployed the field-guns to protect the magazine. They had abandoned the rest of the cantonment to the sepoys' mercy. The *Meerut Gazetteer* remarks on the occurrence of this time:

> "The Judge's court and the tehsildar's office were at once burned down. Mixed crowds of soldiers, sepoys, policemen,

> hangers-on about the bazars, servants and convicts burned and plundered the cantonments, murdering every Christian that they could lay hands on."

It goes on to cite several instances where sepoys as well as civilians saved a number of Europeans. The above occurrence is mentioned in detail in Elisa Greathed's article, '*Normal Account of the Opening of the Indian Mutiny at Meerut*'. Her husband, H. Greathed, was Meerut's commissioner. She has provided a graphic account of her experiences in the Uprising in some detail. She writes that with the onset of the mutiny, violence erupted. Dark had set in a little earlier than usual. Taking advantage of the dark, the revolutionary sepoys plundered arms. A few of them went for the communication facilities, as they knew that this would allow the English to call for help from Delhi. Smoke rose from the direction of the parade ground, and explosions could be heard.

She writes further that she was getting ready for the evening prayers. Listening to the explosions and commotion, the servants shut the doors. It was dark, somewhat lighted by the burning buildings around. Gradually, the gunshots could be heard from very near. She adds that she now knew that the Indian sepoys as well as the civilians had rebelled, and their first targets were the English and imperial symbols. She continues:

> "Mr. Greathed [her husband], after loading his arms, took me to the terrace on the top of the house. . .The increasing tumult, thickening smoke, and fires all around, convinced us of the necessity of making our position as safe as we could; our guard were drawn up below. After dark, a party of insurgents rushed into the grounds, drove off the guard, and broke into the house, and set it on fire. On all sides we could hear them smashing and plundering, and calling loudly for us; it seemed once or twice as though footsteps were on the

> staircase, but no one came up. We owed much to the fidelity of our servants: had but one proved treacherous, our lives must have been sacrificed."

The sentries posted at the bungalow had joined the revolutionaries now, too. The Greatheds had been hiding on the roof for a long time; when they felt everything was safe, they jumped over the rear boundary and went to the area with abundant trees. They hid there for the whole night, looking at the blazing bungalow.

Elisa further writes that the next morning, May 11, they went to the secure area of the cantonment and found no rioting; everything appeared quiet. Some buildings were, of course, burning, and some dead bodies were being removed from the markets. The remaining families and other people had been lodged in the garrisoned depot of the European artillery. She concludes that everything appeared to have died down. In her words:

> "Never was dawn more welcome to us than on the 11th of May; the daylight showed how complete the work of destruction had been. All was turned into ruin and desolation, and our once bright happy home was now a blackened pile. Sad was the scene; but thankfulness for life left no place for other regrets...We had been utterly cut off from all communication through the night, and sad was the tale of murder and bloodshed we now heard, and... it was found that the telegraph wires had been destroyed by the Sepoys, before any knowledge of what was occurring had transpired. The mutineers got away during the night, and pursuit was useless."

This should be in the right context to reveal that the sepoys attacking Elisa's residence belonged to the 11th Infantry Regiment. The English knew it well that they had done injustice to the 85 sepoys, so Colonel Carmichael Smyth, commanding officer of the

3rd Cavalry, as soon as he got the news of the outbreak, kept running from pillar to post to save his life, rather than doing what he was supposed to do—visit his regiment and calm down the sepoys. How scared and bewildered he was can be found out from his own account. Read what he has written:

> "I went first to Mr. Greathed's, gave information to the servants as Mr. G was out. I then went on to the General's, and heard that he had just left the house in his carriage; so I galloped on to the Artillery parade, and found the Brigadier already on the ground; and I accompanied him with the troops to the other end of the cantonments, and remained with him all night."

Quoted by several writers, O'Callaghan has indicted Smyth for his conduct in his *Scattered Chapters on the Indian Mutiny*:

> "I have never been able to discover that the officer commanding the corps repaired to his post, or was seen in the lines amongst his men, during the whole of that eventful evening and night; and it would appear that Colonel Smyth was so fortunate as to make an early escape into the protection of the European military quarter."

Similarly, J.A.B. Palmer, in his book *The Mutiny Outbreak at Meerut in 1857*, says about Smyth that no action was taken against him, 'which lost him some reputation'.

Another interesting anecdote about him is that, the previous evening, when he had received a rumour of an imminent insurrection, he took it as a joke and remarked, "These blacks and uprising, impossible!"

Smyth was not the only Englishman to have received such rumours, but they were so complacent about their power that they felt that the native sepoys could not dare do that, at least in Meerut. Even Lieutenant Hugh had received a report on certain activities in the Sadar Bazar area the previous evening, yet he amazingly kept mum. It is also shocking that the officers noticed the sepoys were unhappy after 85 of them were punished. Yet, no officer tried to soothe their wounds. Not paying attention to rumours proved costly. They had neglected the fact that the native sepoys had been fallen in the parade ground in direct range of the field-guns, and it would have been perilous for them to rise then.

It would be entertaining to remark on the most interesting character among the English officers. It was Major General William Hewitt. Aged about 66 years and with a plump body, he felt more of a drama artist than a military officer. He loved relaxation, so his junior officers little liked him. For him, Sunday was his favourite day; he would not like anything to happen on this day that could disturb his rest.

He had received the report concerning the outbreak, yet he said it was already dark and there was no logic in undertaking the action at that odd hour, so he favoured postponing it to the following morning. This was possibly the reason the native sepoys had encountered no opposition on May 10. To conceal his incapacity, he sent a report to Delhi stating that all European troops were ready in their uniforms as soon as they heard of the Uprising and set out to confront the native sepoys. They first went to the parade ground, but as it was dark, they could not take any action at that time, so they returned to the brigade to protect their barracks and residences. When Brigadier Wilson recommended that Hewitt move back to the brigade for protection, the latter was too happy. Kaye writes tauntingly: "To this, Hewitt, glad to be advised, assented; and the troops set their faces homewards."

The revolutionary sepoys had snapped the telegraph and telephone lines. When information about the Uprising was being sent to Agra, to which Meerut was connected, the wires were cut. The *Meerut Gazetteer* writes:

> "A telegram was sent to Agra, but the wires were cut before the message was completed, and expresses were then sent to Muzaffarnagar, Dehli and Bulandshahr."

Major GW Williams writes in his '*Narrative of Events*' that the rest of the cantonment was completely depopulated. Several native citizens believed that each European had been killed. As none of their power could be seen, they felt that they had been brought under control. The *Meerut Gazetteer* too notes that the British rule had disappeared which spread the belief that every British had been slaughtered. The remaining Europeans feared that the sepoys would return with field-guns to wipe them out completely. Rotton, who was present in Meerut at this time, wrote in his narration:

> "In truth our military authorities were paralysed. No one knew what was best to do, and nothing was accordingly done."

Surendra Nath Sen writes:

> "Never before had the heroic Briton in India felt more helpless and less secure. An insignificant minority in the midst of unfriendly multitude read treachery in every face and suspected treason in every quarter."

There were several instances where the native sepoys saved their British superiors and women. Lieutenant H. Gough (later General) states that he was safely escorted to the artillery lines by a native non-commissioned officer and then left to join his regiment to be part of the Uprising. He recalls in his article *Old Memories* thus:

> "…where having brought me in safety, they made their final salute and left me, notwithstanding my earnest entreaties

and persuasions that they should remain with me,—the native officer averring that his duty was with his regimental comrades, and whether for life or death they must return to their regiment. I never heard again of my friend the native officer. I knew his name of course; but though I found out his house in the Oude district, no trace of him was ever again found, and I could only conclude he met his death at Delhi in the mutineers' camp."

14: On to Delhi

The sepoys did not intend to kill these Englishmen; they attacked only when it was absolutely necessary. They had taken the first step towards driving out the aliens. Now, they reached a point where they could no longer retrace their steps. Having caused upheaval in the church and around it, the sepoys belonging to the 3rd Cavalry started to gather in the parade ground to the south of the nullah. Those of the 20th Regiment were already assembled there, raising slogans. When the cavalrymen revealed to them what they had done, the slogans tore through the sky. Those of the 11th Regiment joined them last, as they were located a little away.

The Uprising had occurred, no doubt, but it was mostly leaderless. The need of the hour was that a capable leader should emerge. The Sanyasi had accomplished the task well, even when he had perceived the sepoys' reluctance; he had created such situations which forced them to pick up arms. It was still at the local level, and it could not have reached its logical outcome without becoming a national movement. The Sanyasi had already planned for that situation.

It was for strange causes that the English had failed miserably to confront the sepoys on May 10, 1857. They could not take any concrete action, but the sepoys knew well that this situation could not last long, as they were quite powerful in Meerut. They were almost equal in numbers and also possessed the magazine, which made them utterly powerful. Having risen, the sepoys had no shelter as they had to abandon their barracks. Now, they were in dire need of an alternative. There was no question of going back, as the English were wont to punish them very harshly even over a trivial mistake, and today they had crossed all limits. To think it over, they were now gathering in the southern part of the nullah. They were enthusiastic, as their success had greatly boosted their confidence.

The entire ground reverberated with the slogans—*Har-Har Mahadev*, *Allah-O-Akbar*, *Deen- Deen*. As yet they seemed to be in different regimental groups. And then like a mighty confluence of the Ganga-Yamuna-Saraswati rivers, they started to form into one whole group. Both Hindu and Muslim sepoys were high in spirit which reflected a grand spectacle of harmony. This was the communal harmony which often scared the English and they made their best attempts to destroy it. Despite their wily efforts, the Hindus and Muslims continued to stand together. Today, it marked the hallmark of their strength.

The sloganeering had commenced with religious overtones, and gradually, other slogans mingled it:

Jo karna hai kar guzro! (Do what you must!)

Do what you must!

One of the groups was louder than the others. It was it round which the sepoys of other regiments crowded. They did not realise that now they all formed part of a larger whole, eradicating their individual identity.

Do what you must!

Do what you must!

Only then did they realise that the Sanyasi was standing in the middle and leading the sloganeering. He seemed to have cast a spell on them all.

"Chalo, chalo, (March, march)," the Sanyasi started a new slogan.

"Chalo, chalo!"

"Dilli chalo! (On to Delhi)."

"Dilli chalo!"

With this was shouted the slogan of 'On to Delhi' for the first time in Indian history, a slogan which will be called in the coming years by several other leaders, the most prominent of them being the legendary Subhash Chandra Bose.

The Sanyasi had taken over the leadership very tactfully. He was transforming their mentality imperceptibly. He was now gradually encouraging them to march to Delhi. He was in command, yet he was not trying to show himself important. His goal was to lead the sepoys to their intended destination and do his best to help the Uprising succeed. He had been working for it for several weeks, so he had no other way but to take full advantage of the opportunity that he had created.

The sepoys had been seeing the Sanyasi near them for quite some time, and now they were able to see his intention clearly. They were raising slogans, and thinking in their heart at the same time that the Uprising had occurred owing to him; they acted only as tools, puppets in his hands.

The Sanyasi had made his plan cleverly, but he wanted the sepoys to think that it was they who were at the helm of everything unfolding there. He gathered the senior sepoys around him and began planning for their next course of action. They were safe only until the English had assessed the actual situation, and this could not occur until the following morning at the earliest. They were not secure in Meerut, but going to Delhi was not without its risks, as the English could somehow transmit the information there. So, even Delhi wasn't very safe for them.

Standing in the middle of the senior sepoys and a few curious new recruits, the Sanyasi said that a good army acted in accordance with the enemy's resources. They, too, had learnt this during their military training. As per the plan for the Uprising on May 31, they were required to move to Delhi. So, it took hardly any time to decide their next move: to march to Delhi. They believed that the native regiments garrisoned there would join them. The Mughal empire had virtually declined, and Bahadur Shah Zafar had little influence even over Delhi, let alone beyond it. Yet, the emperor had his significance, he remained a great symbol of an Indian empire. He could be an effective instrument in spreading the Uprising nationwide. There was a large white army in Delhi, but it was not as powerful as it was in Meerut, as the capital of the East India Company was yet at Calcutta.

With the final decision, the sepoys started to shout slogans once again:

"On to Delhi!"

"On to Delhi!"

It was decided that as the 11th and the 20th were foot regiments, they would take the rural route to Delhi, while the 3rd, being a mounted regiment, would ride to Delhi via the main highway, as the boat bridge across the Hindan in Baghpat would be inadequate for the horses. Moreover, the cavalrymen could easily cover a longer route. They had the advantage of speed, and in case they confronted the British force on the way, they could avoid it easily and speedily, a task that the foot regiments would find harder.

***

They were now ready to act, it was decided that the 85 jailed sepoys should be released. They were unsure which jail they were in, as there was a rumour they might have been transferred to the old jail. There were two jails in Meerut then—an old jail near

Kesarganj, usually used for criminals, and the new jail near Suraj Kund, which was demolished later in 1866 to build Victoria Park. It is this place where the Memorial stands to commemorate the Uprising and where annual celebration programmes related to the 1857 Uprising are held. It is the same ground where, a century later, in November 1946, the Congress Session was held, which passed the resolution to constitute the Constituent Assembly for independent India.

These jails were located in the opposite direction, so the 3rd Cavalry was assigned the task of relieving the incarcerated comrades, who, coincidentally, were their buddies too. Finally, the footmen, led by the Sanyasi, headed to Delhi, while the cavalrymen turned their horses towards Kesarganj via Police Street, near Sadar Bazar. At the jail, they learned that their comrades had never been brought there, so they turned towards the new jail. They had to be careful as the artillery brigade was quite near this destination. They were ready to meet any eventuality, but fortunately, they did not. The jail seemed geared up to receive the deliverers. The native jail guards had not participated in the Uprising until then and were still doing their duty. They not only assisted the visitors, but also joined them march to Delhi.

The keys to the cells were in the jailor's possession, who was not present at that hour. As a result, the walls' edges were broken to remove the iron bars and bring out the prisoners. As they were yet in fetters, ironsmiths had to be brought in, which took some time before they could be freed completely. As the wait lengthened, anxiety pervaded the atmosphere, as there could be an attack by the English. However, they seemed to be backstage, nursing their wounds. Finishing their work, all sepoys quickly rode away, two riding a horse each, to join their comrades. It should be pertinent to mention that the sepoys freed only their 85 comrades, and none of the other criminals or prisoners, who were later freed in an attack by the villagers. The *Meerut Gazetteer* reports this in these words:

> "Meantime a large party of the 3rd Cavalry rushed to the jail and released their comrades without the slightest opposition from the jail guard or the guard of the 20th Native Infantry. None of the other convicts were released by the troopers, nor were the persons or property of the European jailor and his family molested. The prisoners, to the number of 839, were let out by a mob of villagers who, emboldened by impunity, attacked, broke open and set fire to the jail about midnight."

The *Meerut Gazetteer* similarly notes that, at another place, 720 inmates of the old jail were later set free by mobs.

There is no record or evidence to show what happened to these 85 sepoys after this. We, of course, know their names, and nothing further is known about them. The only information about them is that the Hindu sepoys came from the Awadh region, while the Muslim sepoys came from part of the Punjab today known as Haryana. They were now a few of those nationalists who had bidden their lives for the supreme sacrifice. The blood of these warriors has irrigated the land that has emerged as India, that is Bharat, today.

The fact remains that not all native sepoys had taken part in the Uprising, as those under the command of Lieutenant Mackenzie did not take part in it, nor did those posted in the magazine. Those posted in the treasury securely handed over the charge before joining their comrades in arms.

The truth remains that several mysteries have remained

unresolved in the absence of evidence and records; much is based on conjecture. Our protagonist Sanyasi is also wrapped in mystery, we have been able to enunciate his role to a great extent with help from the circumstantial evidence.

***

It was completely dark. In the upheaval today, no one had lit the kerosene oil lamps at the gate or elsewhere. In the dim moonlight, men looked more like silhouettes. The plan to march to Delhi was final. The footmen had to move right then, while the remaining sepoys of the 3rd Cavalry had to wait for their men to return from the jail.

A sepoy called, "A marker is needed who can lead us."

The Sanyasi said at once, "It's I here. Follow me." With this, he set off with long strides, and the sepoys went after him with their heavy-sounding steps, soon turning on the narrow muddy path in the wooded area, presently Rohta Road. For the first time, the sepoys noticed that the Sanyasi held a lantern emitting dim light. The moon seemed to move with the moving party.

Not far they had gone when a sepoy caught up with the Sanyasi and said, "Baba, how do you know of this route?"

"I've walked this route several times," said the Sanyasi as he further picked up pace. "Why...what made you do that?" The sepoy's curiosity was at its highest.

"As you had to be guided to Delhi one or the other day," said the Sanyasi with a mysterious smile that went unnoticed in the dark.

Several writers have described the Sanyasi leading the sepoys to Delhi on foot through the rural route. Even today, you can find this route covered in dense greenery, while the population has grown several times over, and many of the present-day villages did not yet exist. We can guess that the entire area was then more like a dense forest. It was important that the sepoys did not lose their way as they had to cross the path in pitch dark in an area they knew nothing about. The Sanyasi was like a glimmer of hope for them in this darkness.

The Sanyasi walked as if he knew the route well. He must have realised that the sepoys had been on their toes since the evening, and they must be tired as well as hungry. Most of them would not have eaten anything after lunch. Hunger and fatigue, too, are types of sacrifice which they were making now. Soon, the party abandoned the muddy path and took the paved road towards Barnawa, bypassing Sardhana. It was the same village believed to have the well-known Lakshagraha, or wax palace, as mentioned in the Mahabharata, which the Kaurava princes built to burn down the Pandava princes. Touching its outer periphery, they turned towards Panchli Buzurg. It was the village in which the English would take brutal revenge for disobedience in a few days. They moved at a uniform pace as they negotiated with muddy walkways, grassy pathways and paved roads. The unwavering Sanyasi traversed as if he were used to walking there.

Soon it was midnight. In the sky, the clouds seemed to play hide-and-seek with the moon. When the clouds cleared, a silvery moon would shower its dim light over the area, helping the sepoys realise the truth of the silhouettes formed by the trees and other structures. They had just turned from near the village when a youth on a bullock cart started to distribute mangoes. When enquired what he was doing there at that odd hour, he said that he was waiting for the dawn to take his crop of mangoes to the market, but they could better serve the hungry revolutionaries. One mango was not enough; rather, it had aroused their hunger. Anyway, something was better than nothing.

The sepoys were amazed when the villagers in Baleni started distributing chapatis and vegetables wrapped in leafy rolls. They were now sure that the news of the Uprising had reached far and wide. It enthused them, further firming their resolve. They got some food in Bijrol too. They were pleasantly surprised to learn that the villagers were repairing the almost-broken bridge between Baleni and Bijrol. In the coming days, Shahmal, the resident of Bijrol, would confront the English with his large farming army and make the supreme sacrifice. They trod the path via Daula, Tatiri and Kattha on the way to Baghpat. When they crossed Khekra to reach the outskirts of Loni, it was about three in the morning. They were fully tired, but sensing Delhi in their easy reach, just 8 miles away, they moved on. Khajuri Khas was the last village on their route, and then they would have to face the main impediment: the mighty Yamuna River.

As they walked towards it, the eastern sky glowed in glorious red, as if welcoming them and congratulating them on the feat they had accomplished. The water could be smelled in the air, beckoning that the river was quite near. They arrived at the Yamuna bank with the first rays of the sun. They had walked all night, that too on muddy and unpaved pathways through villages, farms and forests. They were fatigued, for sure, yet they did not feel it much, as they were enthusiastic about what they had achieved. With the wide river with gurgling waters before them, they were delighted to the extreme. Across the river stood the Red Fort; despite its historical glory, it seemed somewhat subdued, as if it were tired of waiting for someone—maybe it was waiting for these sepoys who had now shown up across the rapid currents to liberate it.

The Sanyasi, too, asked the sepoys for water. They not only drank but also washed their hands and feet. A couple of them removed their clothes and jumped into it. The wide river was full of rapidly moving currents as it had already started raining in the mountains. The Sanyasi suggested that they should cross the river by the boat bridge. It often broke due to rapid currents and wind, but it was lucky to see it in a serviceable condition. It was windy, causing a swift current in the water, which made the middle part of the bridge sway violently; this could pose a grave challenge to pedestrians on it. As a result, the sepoys had to cross the middle section on all fours. It was part of their training, but they were amazed to find that the Sanyasi was no less skilled than they were at this type of crawling.

When they all had landed safely on the other side, the Sanyasi asked them to move towards the Lahori Gate along the moat. At the kerb before the turn stood their comrades from the 3rd Cavalry waiting, who had reached much before and were alert. They appeared more numerous than they ought to be. Maybe some sepoys from Delhi had already joined them.

The fact was this. When the 3rd Cavalry reached the Red Fort, the sepoys posted there decided to cooperate with them. Not only this, they planned to chase away the English immediately; after which they entered the city, went towards Darya Ganj, and attacked any Englishman they found. They erased English-signs and set several buildings occupied by foreigners on fire. Commissioner Frazer tried to obstruct them, but he paid with his life. Others, too, met the same fate. It seemed impossible to restrain the enthusiastic sepoys.

The previous evening, the sepoys had destroyed the communication lines, yet the English were able to deliver a message to Delhi, suggesting that the revolutionary sepoys might head there and contact Bahadur Shah Zafar. When Colonel Ripley, commanding officer of the 54th Native Regiment, garrisoned at the Red Fort, received this information, he surmised that they could approach the old Mughal ruler there to request his leadership. He posted his regiment just inside the Lahori Gate, extending in a column through the Chhatta Chowk. He had a couple of field batteries, which now stood in the small ground facing the gate. All his native men were alert and ready. He had posted a company of sepoys on the ramparts; this was why the sepoys from Meerut stood at the kerb, but were now ready to enter the gate. Will a violent skirmish take place there? Will a native regiment attack another? Equipped with cannons and secure structures, the 54th seemed to be in an advantageous position. Could it mean that the Meerut revolutionaries were destined to be sacrificed in one sweep of the grapeshot? The questions were difficult, and the response was just moments away.

As soon as some of the revolutionary sepoys entered the small gate, Ripley ordered his men to be alert. The guards straightened their muskets. Finding themselves at the mercy of the muskets and cannons, the visiting sepoys were alarmed; they turned to the followers to wait in a commotion when Ripley screamed aloud: "Fire!" He was dumbstruck to see his sepoys standing motionless like statues. He repeated his command, this time with all his energy. And then the first shot was fired; it was the only gunshot. With this was heard a heart-rending cry from one who had received the bullet. It was none other than Ripley who had fallen victim to it. With his breath leaving him and falling on his back, his open eyes expressed shock when he found the opponent sepoys saluting one another; this expression did not fade even after they turned stony. As a report goes, Ripley had said to his fellow officers that the sepoys of his own regiments had bayoneted him.

With this, the fort's main gate was thrown open. The sepoys entered, and so did many civilians, everyone raising slogans. They occupied the fort and headed immediately to the Khas Mahal as they wished to meet Bahadur Shah Zafar in person. The personal guard, Captain Douglas, tried to restrain them, but he was pushed aside. He escaped with his life without uttering a word. The rapidly unfolding events had taken even the Mughal ruler by surprise. He, too, heard of the likely Uprising on May 31, but it was still three weeks away. He consulted his advisors and decided to meet the revolutionaries. He appeared through the perforated marble screen of his Khas Mahal, under which the sepoys had gathered.

The sepoys reported to the Mughal ruler that the English had been beaten at Meerut and had been pushed back even in Delhi. They desired that he take over the reins of the Uprising.

"Even if I get ready to accept the leadership, I have no money to pay you any salary. My treasury is as good as empty," Zafar expressed his helplessness.

"We'll present you with the English treasury," said the sepoys.

With this, Bahadur Shah Zafar assented to be the leader. The sepoys said to him, "We would like to honour you."

They wanted to bestow honour on the new leader by the hand of the Sanyasi, who they thought was the harbinger of the Uprising. They looked for him here and there. No one remembered if he had entered the fort at all. They did not know when he had disappeared from amongst them. Maybe his goal had been accomplished. No one knew his name; they called him Aughar Baba. They did not know where he had come from and where he had gone. There was no time to think about him; rather, they had to focus on the Uprising and spread it further. They all wanted to establish a pan-India empire, and not small states here and there. Their resolve was clearly expressed in their loud slogans – *Hail Emperor Subedar Sipahi Bahadur of Hindustan!*

Zafar was in action as soon as he took up the reins of the

Uprising. He sent his messengers to the magazine near the fort to surrender. Kaye notes:

> ". . .a summons came to them [defenders] in the name of the King. . .Again and again, messengers came from the Palace saying that His Majesty had ordered the gates to be opened, and the stores given up to the Army."

The sepoys stepped out of the Red Fort. Their strength was rapidly rising. The 38th and the 74th Native Regiments had joined them, and the English had lost control over Delhi. All this had occurred in just a few hours. The artillery was yet under the English control, with one magazine just near the fort. They planned and advanced to it. Sometime later, it was destroyed in a massive explosion.

The sepoys seemed to have forgotten the Sanyasi for the time being, as they had more important tasks to undertake. However, it is the opportune moment to reveal the protagonist Sanyasi's identity, who played a vital role in the Uprising.

15: The Harbinger's Identity and Evidence

What was the real identity of our protagonist– the Sanyasi, who brought on the Uprising? Who was the great soul who initiated such a massive revolution in which millions of lives were sacrificed? Who was he who had forced the so-called invincible English to run helter-skelter like a terrorised lamb? Who was he whose effort culminated in the end of the East India Company's rule? You will be amazed to learn who this great personality was; you will hardly believe that it was he and no one else. He was indeed a great personality. If a list of the ten all-time greatest people of India is made, his name will certainly find a mention in it.

Our protagonist was none other than Dayanand – Swami Dayanand Saraswati. If you ever doubt our claim, please read on.

All those historians and scholars who have worked on the 1857 Uprising can be divided into two classes: first, those who negate any of Swami Dayanand's role in the Uprising; and second, those who raise illogical points to prove his role in it. If these two diverse, contradictory doctrines are analysed, several interesting facts emerge.

To research the role of Swami Dayanand in the 1857 Uprising, we have visited several places, met and spoken with several historians and scholars, and consulted several texts and books. On the basis of these sources, we have been able to infer his role in the massive Uprising.

Let us first consider the arguments of those who negate any role of Swami Dayanand in this Uprising. They all state the same point: there is no such evidence that points to his contribution. Most of these historians have undertaken no research in this respect and have even shied away from commenting on this topic. Not only this, but most of such claimants have not read his biography, which is quite concise. Only a few historians have negated his role in it, as BK Singh in his book, *Swami Dayanand* (in Hindi). He writes:

> "He had seen the 1857 Uprising fail with his own eyes, he knew well that freedom could not be attained unless the Indian society was reformed fully. And this task could not be accomplished in a year or two. It needed a long-term and conscious effort in which all segments of the society needed to make respective contributions. It is imprudent to say that Swami Dayanand had a role of any type in the 1857 revolt. Some people still state that he had a specific role in the 1857 revolt. There is no historical evidence in support of this opinion. Nor is there any fact which can point to this. He was engaged in the discovery of 'truth' those days."

BK Singh's argument can well be confronted by what he himself states. He says that Swami Dayanand had witnessed the 1857 Uprising fail with his own eyes. If he 'was engaged in the discovery of truth those days' in the dense forest near the origin of the Narmada, how could he see the revolt fail? In addition, there are several facts and pieces of evidence which point to his role in the 1857 Uprising; of course, they are not direct indications of his role, but there is no dearth of circumstantial evidence. We shall come to them soon.

The scholars and historians who deny Swami Dayanand's role in it also cite his biography. The fun is that there are conflicting views about his biography. As we have told you earlier, there are three biographies attributed to him, which he narrated on three occasions: at Pune, in *The Theosophist*, and at Calcutta. The first two of these are unanimously acknowledged, and, more interestingly, only one – the second – is considered authentic. The very existence of the third, the most detailed one, is denied and even described as dubious, suspicious, fake and untrustworthy.

Swami Dayanand did not wish to reveal all about himself; however, as he grew popular, the number of his followers increased, and many ardently curious people would often ask him about his personal life. Following such repetitive entreaties, he narrated his life for the first time at Pune (Maharashtra) on August 4, 1875. In it, he briefly described his life from birth to the establishment of the Arya Samaj. This narration was published in contemporary newspapers; on the basis of these news reports, his biography was written. The existence of this biography is universally acknowledged; however, it is not considered fully authentic, as some vital details are missing. But the same is true of all his biographies.

For the second time, he got his biography published in a periodical named '*The Theosophist*' in the year 1879-80. This biography is accepted as authentic, yet it is not fully free from controversy. Before we deal with it in detail, we are inclined to discuss the third occasion, *Calcutta Text*, which has attracted the severest criticism and censure.

Some sources claim that, in addition to the two occasions quoted above, Swami Dayanand narrated his biography on yet another occasion: in 1872-73, when he stayed in the province of Bengal for four months. He stayed in Calcutta from December 16, 1872, to April 16 of the following year. It was here that several prominent people met him, including leaders of the Brahmo Samaj (Mahrishi Debendranath Thakur, Keshabchandra Sen and others), thinkers and social reformers (like Ishwar Chandra

Vidyasagar), litterateurs (Rameshchandra Dutta ICS) and many others. It is also claimed that Debendranath Thakur, Ishwar Chandra Vidyasagar, and Keshabchandra Sen appointed some writers with profound knowledge of Sanskrit to put into writing all of Dayanand's sermons and narrations, as he did not know Bengali and therefore spoke in Sanskrit. It is claimed that he narrated his life in ten days in March 1873.

The very existence of these narrations is denied; none was aware of what happened to these writings, but rumours about these papers circulated. It was due to this that Dayanand's biographer, Pt. Lekhram Aryapathik tried to locate these papers but was unsuccessful, so he noted in the biography that, in 1872, Dayanand was requested to tell about his life, but to no avail. He concluded this topic thus:

> "Some respectable gentlemen endeavoured to know the details of his life, yet failed. Dayanand would tell some anecdotes before scholarly hermits out of friendship, but he considered it meaningless to tell such things before the ordinary householders."

In 1923, Pandit Deenbandhu Vedshastri learned of Swami Dayanand's biographical lecture delivered during his sojourn at Calcutta, which was translated into Bengali by various Sanskrit scholars; of these papers, some were here and others there. He worked in a mission mode to gather these papers and succeeded for a number of them, and then compiled them in the *Sarvadeshik* magazine titled '*Mahrishi Dayanand Saraswati Ki Agyat-Jeevani*' (Unknown Biography of the Sage Dayanand Saraswati). These articles were published in 66 instalments between January 5, 1969, and November 8, 1970. Later, these articles were published in a book form titled '*Yogi Ka Atma-Charitra*' (Autobiography of a Yogi), for which Swami Sachchidanand Saraswati made an effort. This biography is also known as the *Calcutta Text*.

Some of the anecdotes mentioned in the *Calcutta Text*, which are considered hard to believe, include his confrontation with bears, lions, and snakes that brought him no harm. This is, of course, true that a few incidents mentioned in it can be remotely corroborated by his statements, forming part of his sermons delivered at different places on different occasions, or by his statements forming part of his treatises. These facts, taken together, make this biography somewhat mysterious, unbelievable, and refutable.

This biography, moreover, claims that Dayanand forbade its publication during his lifetime. It is but natural to cast aspersions on this type of claim; however, this claim cannot be called illogical, as the fact of his role in the revolution would have been the cause of a calamitous consequence. The English had not spared anyone found to be directly or indirectly involved in the great Uprising; not only this, when a person from a village was found to be involved, the entire village had to suffer the appalling consequences, as it did in a large number of instances.

Thus, of the three biographies about Swami Dayanand's life, the existence of the first one (*Pune Text*) is accepted; the second one (*The Theosophist* one) is acknowledged as authentic; and the third one (*Calcutta Text*) is taken as false.

Now, let us take up the biography for analysis, which is accepted as authentic and credible. Upon reading, you will find it quite vague. It was published in English in a periodical called '*The Theosophist*', published by the Theosophical Society. It speaks in a roundabout manner; wherever it can, it deviates from the main discussion and hides facts. It describes even small, insignificant occurrences and indefinite periods, yet shies away from stating important occurrences and periods. If this has been the approach, there must have been some special reasons, and we would like to delve into them. An extract of this biography, pertaining specifically to the period of the 1857 Uprising, goes thus:

> "Having lingered for some time on the banks of the Ganges, I arrived next at Farrukhabad, when, just as having passed Sreenjeerma [Srangirampur] I was entering Cawnpore by the road east of the cantonment, the Samvat year 1912 [on April 5, 1856 A.D.] was completed.
>
> "During the following five months, I visited many a place between Cawnpore and Allahabad. In the beginning of Bhadrapad, I arrived at Mirzapur where I stopped for a month or so near the shrine of Brindachal Asoolasjee [Vindhiachal Asoolasji]; and, arriving at Benaras in the early part of Ashwin, I took my quarters in the cave (at the confluence of the Baruna and the Ganges) which then belonged to Bhunanda Saraswati. There, I met with Kakaram, Rajaram and other Shastrees, but stopped there only for twelve days and renewed my travels <u>after what I sought for</u>. It was at the shrine of Durga-koho in Chandalgurh [now known as Chunar] where I passed ten days, that I left off eating rice altogether, and living but on milk, I gave myself up entirely to the study of Yog, which I practised night and day."

Before proceeding, I would like to remark on the words in the previous paragraph that I have underlined. These words explicitly describe Swami Dayanand's firm resolve to study grammar and the Vedas, for which he was seeking an able teacher. Is it possible that, soon after expressing his determination, he would deviate from his path of finding a teacher? If we carefully study his personality and character, we find that this is utterly impossible. Please read further:

> "Unfortunately, I got into the habit of using *bhang*—a

strong narcotic leaf—and at times felt quite intoxicated with its effects. Once, leaving the temple, I came to a village near Chandalgurh, where I met with an attendant of mine of former days. On the other side of the village, and at some distance, stood a Sivalaya [a temple of Shiva] whither I proceeded to pass the night under its walls. While there, under the influence of *bhang*, I fell fast asleep and dreamt that night a dream. . .I thought I saw Mahadeo and his wife Parvati. They were conversing together and the subject of their talk was myself. Parvati was telling Mahadeo that I ought to get married, but the god did not agree with her. She pointed to the *bhang*. . .The dream annoyed me a good deal when I awoke. It was raining and I took shelter on the veranda opposite the chief entrance to the temple, where stood the huge statue of the Bull-god Nandi. Placing my books and clothes on its back I sat and meditated; when suddenly happening to throw a look inside the statue which was empty, I saw a man concealed inside. I extended my hand towards him, and must have terrified him, as, jumping out of his hiding-place, he took to his heels in the direction of the village. Then I crept into the statue in my turn and slept there for the rest of the night. In the morning an old woman came and worshipped the Bull-god with myself inside. Later on, she returned with offerings of "Gur" (molasses) and a pot of "Dahi" [curd milk] which, making Puja to me, she offered and desired me to accept and eat. I did not disabuse her: but being hungry, ate it all. The curd being very sour proved a good antidote for the *bhang* and dispelled all signs of intoxication, which relieved me very much.

"I then continued my journey towards the hills where the Nerbudda [Narmada River] takes its rise."

What needs to be noted is that after mentioning this specific date (the completion of the Samvat year of 1912, which was April 5, 1856), Swami Dayanand does not tell anything substantial, but limits himself to describing the jungle or his adventures in it, trying to make believe as if he were in the jungles near Narmada. However, in the very previous paragraph, he explicitly states that he was in a village near Chandalgarh (Chunar). The two places are over 400 kilometres apart, and he does not tell how and when he covered this distance. Obviously, it is an attempt to conceal a vital fact:

> "I never once asked my way, but went on travelling southward. Soon I found myself in a desolate spot covered thickly with jungles, with isolated huts appearing now and then among the bushes at irregular distances. At one of such places I drank a little milk and proceeded onward. . .But about half a mile further, I came to a dead stop. The road had abruptly disappeared and there remained but the choice of narrow paths leading I knew not where. I soon entered a dreary jungle of wild plum trees and very thick and huge grass with no signs of any path in it, when suddenly I was faced by a huge black bear. The beast growled ferociously, and, rising on its hind legs, opened wide its mouth to devour me. . .I stood motionless for some time and then slowly raised my thin cane over him. . . and, the bear ran away terrified. So loud was its roaring that the villagers whom I had just left, hearing it, ran to my assistance and soon appeared armed with large sticks and followed by their dogs. They tried hard to persuade me to return with them. If I proceeded any farther, they said, I would have to encounter the greatest perils in the jungles which in those hills were the habitant of bears, buffaloes, elephants, tigers and other

ferocious beasts. I asked them not to feel anxious for my safety, for I was protected. I was anxious to see the sources of the Nerbudda, and would not change my mind for fear of any peril. Then seeing that their warnings were useless, they left me after having made me accept a stick thicker than my own for 'self-defence' they said, which stick I immediately threw away.

"On that day I travelled without stopping until it grew quite dusk. For long hours I had not perceived the slightest trace of human habitation around me, no villages in the far off, not even a solitary hut, or a human being. But what my eyes met the most, was a number of trees, twisted and broken, which had been uprooted by the wild elephants and felled by them to the ground, obstructed the already difficult passage. Still further on, I found myself in a dense and impenetrable jungle of plum trees and other prickly shrubs, whence, at first, I saw no means of extricating myself. However, partly crawling on the belly, partly creeping on my knees, I conquered this new obstacle and after paying a heavy tribute with pieces of my clothes and even my own skin, bleeding and exhausted I got out of it. It had grown quite dark by that time, but even this—if it impeded—did not arrest my progress onward, and I still proceeded, until I found myself entirely hemmed in by lofty rocks and hills thickly grown over with dense vegetation, but with evident signs of being inhabited.

"Soon I perceived a few huts, surrounded by heaps of cowdung, a flock of goats grazing on the banks of a small stream of clear water and a few welcome lights glimmering between the crevices of the walls. Resolving to pass the night there, and to go no farther till the next morning, I took

> shelter at the foot of a large tree which overshadowed one of the huts. Having washed my bleeding feet, my face and hands in the stream, I had barely sat to read my prayers, when I was suddenly disturbed in my meditations by the loud sounds of tom-tom. Shortly after, I saw a procession of men, women and children, followed by their cows and goats, emerging from the huts and preparing for a night religious festival. Upon perceiving a stranger, they all gathered around me, and an old man came enquiring from whence I had appeared. I told them I had come from Benaras, and was on my pilgrimage to Nerbudda sources, after which answer they all left me to my prayers, and went further on. But in about half an hour, came one of their headmen accompanied by two hill-men and sat by my side. He came as a delegate to invite me to their huts. But, as before, I refused the offer. He then ordered a large fire to be lit near me and appointed two men to watch over my safety the whole night. Learning that I used milk for my food, the kind headsman asked for my "kamandalu" (ewer) and brought it back to me full of milk, of which I drank a little that night. He then retired, leaving me under the protection of my two guards. That night I soundly slept until dawn, when rising and having completed my devotions, I prepared myself for further events."

It is here that the biography ends abruptly. If you read the final two paragraphs closely, you will find several anomalies: first, in a bid to prove that he was proceeding to the Narmada's origin on a certain date, he has lengthened the description with insignificant details, which is not the case elsewhere, though he has described himself as being in Chandalgarh just a few lines before. Despite its length, it tells nothing substantial. Second, he claims to be proceeding to the Narmada source, but never describes it, even though he says he was there for three years doing Yoga. Third, he admits having stayed at Hindu shrines with installed idols. He specifically mentions a Shivalaya in Chandalgarh, where he stayed for the night and also partook of the offerings. Yet a few paragraphs later, he says he declined the hillmen's invitation, presumably because they were idolaters. With such inconsistencies and this kind of approach, it is but natural for questions to arise. Without answering these questions in depth, it would be hard to reach any conclusion about his role in the 1857 Uprising.

There is more to this biography. To get it published in *The Theosophist* journal, Dayanand had it written in three instalments by his writer, to be sent to the journal's presidents, Colonel H.S. Olcott and Madam Blavatsky. The first of these was published in the monthly in its inaugural edition of October 1879, from pages 9-12, under the column '*Arya Prakash*'. This biographical account was got translated into English by Dayanand. Probably Munshi Samarthadan rendered it into English, who also got other articles published in this magazine.

Commenting on the quality of this translation, Max Muller stated: "Some doubts, however, have been thrown on the correctness of the English rendering of that paper. . ." Later, he remarked in his book *Auld Lang Syne* (*My Indian Friends*) thus:

> "The life of Dayananda published under the authority of the so-called Theosophists, which I accepted formerly as genuine, has been discredited, and we shall probably never have a real biography of the man, for biography in India seems to share the fate of history; either it tells us nothing or what it tells us is fact and fiction so mixed together that it is impossible to separate the one from the other."

The second instalment of the biography was published, not in the following month, but in December 1879. The third instalment appeared in the magazine after a prolonged interval until November 1880.

There occurred some other events during this interval that a person needs to know to draw a proper inference. During this interval, Swami Dayanand grew unhappy with the other materials being included in the journal, especially as they showed that Olcott and Blavatsky were atheists and Buddhists, ultimately leading to the separation of the two institutions. The third instalment was probably given to Olcott by Dayanand himself, and there is no record regarding it. It is this instalment of the biography that seems to have been tampered with.

When we point out this tampering or manipulation, it becomes incumbent upon others to know some facts. Throughout his biography, from childhood onward, Dayanand does not mention any definite dates; he only indicates the year of his birth as Samvat 1881 and the year of abandoning home as Samvat 1903. When he visited the Kumbha Fair, he referred to Samvat 1911. The other dates cannot be determined accurately, even if his description is taken as the basis. This is the reason that even his date of birth is a subject of speculation among scholars. In most places, he describes an indefinite period, as he stayed at one place for two months and at another for ten or a few days.

And then, as if realisation dawns at one place, he mentions a specific date, a date on which he set out to undertake a journey. The important point is that he has not achieved any specific goal on this date. The moot point is: Why does he wish to tell this date? It is after this specific date that his biography ends abruptly, without any conclusion. Another question that pertains to this abrupt interruption is: What happened to his goal for which he was wandering from place to place? That was to find a Guru. He had not yet found one, yet he claimed that he went to the origin of the Narmada to practise Yoga, which he had learnt for six years at Ahmedabad and Mount Abu just before going to Haridwar to attend the Kumbh, and had been practising it ever since. He has expressly said in his *The Theosophist* biography that he practised Yoga even in Haridwar. In his words:

> "Still later, it was divulged to me that there were many far higher and more learned Yogis than those I had hitherto met, yet still not the highest, who resided on the peaks of the mountain of Aboo, in Rajputana. Thither then, I travelled again to visit such noted places of sanctity as the Aarvada Bhawanee and others; encountering at last, those who I so eagerly sought for, on the peak of Bhawanee Giree, and learning from them various other systems and modes of Yoga. It was in the year of Samvat 1911, that I first joined in the Kumbha Mella at Hardwar, where so many sages and divine philosophers meet, often unperceived, together. So long as the Mella congregation of pilgrims lasted, I kept practising that science in the solitude of the jungle of Chandee; and after the pilgrims had separated, I transferred myself to Rhusheekesh [Rishikesh] where sometimes in the company of good and pure Yogis and Sanyasis, oftener alone, I continued in the study and practise of Yoga."

The most amazing fact is that in other sources, the next description is dated as 1860 AD, when he goes to see his Guru Swami Virajanand. There is no conclusive or historical proof about this three-year period, beginning a little before 1857 and ending in 1860; this is the period during which the well-known Uprising of 1857 took place, which lasted until 1859. A pertinent question arises: Will a person, who was ardently seeking a teacher to learn grammar from so that he could study Vedas and other philosophical texts, go into dense forests to practise Yoga, which he had already learnt and which he had been practising all along, rather than to go and see the teacher about whom he had come to know? From this scenario arises the doubt that Swami Dayanand has created confusion in all his biographies only to conceal his involvement in the 1857 Uprising, which was raging in full fury at the time.

Another of his autobiographies is Poona Text, which he narrated on August 4, 1875, and was written down based on news reports. All scholars accept its existence. A plain reading of it reveals that it is equally vague in nature. Have a look:

> "From there [Ahmedabad] I walked on to Haridwar. At that time, the Kumbh Fair was on. From there, I went to the place from where the Alaknanda rises. It was all snow there with the water being extremely cold. Something in the water hurt my foot causing a wound and bleeding. I wished that I would give up my body here in the Himalayas. Then a thinking, however, dawned on me that the body ought to be relinquished only after the wisdom was attained. Determining this, I came to Mathura. I met a saintly hermit. His name was Virajanand Swami. Earlier he lived in Alwar. He was 81 years of age then. He had a profound aptitude in Vedas and other Aryan scriptures. He was blind in both eyes and suffered from stomachache. He did not like the modern *Kaumidi-Shekhar* and other texts. He bitterly criticised the *Puranas* like the *Bhagwat*. He had extreme devotion to all Aryan scriptures. As I introduced myself to him, he intimated that grammar could be learnt in three years, so I decided to study under him. There was a gentleman named Amarlal in Mathura. I cannot forget the favour he did for me during my study period. He made a good arrangement

> of books and meals. If he was ever required to go out, he would feed me first before leaving. He was a person of a really benevolent attitude.
>
> "Having finished my study, I stayed at Agra for two years, but I kept in touch with Swamiji through personal meetings or correspondence in order to resolve my doubts."

While in *The Theosophist* text, Swami Dayanand claims that he went around several places along the Ganga to finally head to the Narmada origin; in the *Poona Text*, on the contrary, he states that he went from Haridwar to Mathura almost directly, and this could not have taken him more time than a couple of months to be in the guardianship of Swami Virajanand for study. The underlined words in the above quote again show his firm determination to seek wisdom.

If, for a while, we also accept the existence of the *Calcutta Text*, we are amazed to find yet another story unfolding in it, in which he claims to have visited a large number of places in South India during this period.

When there are three autobiographies and all of which tell a different tale, there is every reason to doubt that the narrator is trying to hide something vital on one or the other pretext. This is the reason that the circumstantial evidence about his participation in the 1857 Uprising becomes vital to prove his role in it. There can be no doubt that he was trying to sweep under the carpet the truth of his participation in the great revolution because it could mar his very mission, the goal for which he had worked hard and travelled wide. If he ever acquiesced to his role in the Uprising, it would have deprived him, at the hands of the English masters, the opportunity to accomplish his primary goal of attaining and spreading wisdom among the masses. The English rulers were notorious for unleashing the cruellest vengeance upon anyone who was even suspected of having participated in the Uprising. This would have impeded the attainment of his aspiration totally.

Does this fact not imply that Swami Dayanand wished to conceal his role in the Uprising? He himself has stated that a lower goal can be sacrificed for the attainment of a higher goal, and this appears to be the case here. We find numerous such instances in our history; for instance, when Shivaji escaped from the Mughal ruler Aurangzeb's prison, he assigned the security of his son Sambhaji to a Brahmin called Vishwasrao in Mathura and proceeded to Pune alone. This Brahmin had never told a lie all his life and considered it the gravest sin. Upon suspicion, the Mughal troops approached his residence for an enquiry; at this, he simply refused to admit that Sambhaji was with him, describing the young prince as his relative. After the troops left, his wife confronted him about why he had committed such a sin, which had destroyed all his good deeds. In response, the Brahmin said that a lower, inferior goal could be sacrificed for the attainment of a higher, superior goal. Such a lie is not a sin, nor is it untruth. There are several such exceptions mentioned in the Vedas, which logically justify conduct otherwise considered wrong. Such exceptions include even flesh-eating. We are alluding to these references because he had unwavering faith in the Vedic literature and Hindu history.

Swami Dayanand was faced with a similar conundrum. The higher, superior goal before him was to propagate the Vedic virtue and to realise people's emancipation. It was a time when Hinduism was under vicious attacks, which moved him to the innermost being. His magnum opus, *Satyartha Prakash*, is replete with such instances, and he wished to protect his faith from these threats, which, for him, was the superior goal. He surmised that complete freedom could not be attained without awakening the masses.

This was why he did not wish to take part in any freedom struggle without having performed the basic task. However, he faced a situation in which two Gurus, capable of helping him achieve the higher goal, asked him, one after another, to first participate in the planned insurrection. Seeing no other way but join the struggle; he made up his mind to be part of it and pledged to play an important role in the eruption of the revolution.

Even before he assented to taking part in the Uprising, he knew that it was destined to fail. He had wandered across the country and knew well the balance of power between the native people and the English. He felt that the revolution could not succeed, even if it were started, when the rulers of the princely states believed they were the vanquished race. Even if a few of the rulers rose against the imperialist English, the revolution was bound to fail. His works clearly enunciate this fact.

It is also certain that any admission by Swami Dayanand of his role in the Uprising would bring a bitter vengeance at the hands of the English, and this could not be limited to him personally; rather, all those people and organisations, including the Arya Samaj, would have suffered massively, and the superior goal would have fallen in an irredeemable state. For him, the superior goal was to realise a progressive society that could lead the country towards freedom, and admitting his role in the revolution could have proved only an impediment to realising this goal.

In the eleventh *Samullas* or chapter of *Satyartha Prakash*, Swami Dayanand writes:

> "When in Samvat 1914 the English struck at the temple idols, where did the idols go? The Bagher people fought bravely and defeated the enemy, but the idol could not break even a housefly's leg. If there were someone of the like of Sri Krishna, he would have taken the better of the enemy

who would flee helter-skelter. There is nothing ill in saying if the protector is being beaten, his refugees are sure to be thrashed."

It is also worth noting that this statement did not appear in the first edition of the book; in the second edition, Swami Dayanand himself inserted it. It would be proper to remark on his language proficiency. He was a Gujarati with an absolute command of Gujarati and Sanskrit. Yet, he wrote all his literature in Hindi to connect with countrymen across regions. It is also true that he did not have complete command of Hindi in the early stages of his public life, as is clear from his works. Thus, he has played a leading role in establishing Hindi as the link language in the country.

The above extract proves that he did not think that in Samvat 1914 (1857 AD), people were ready for any revolution. Having finished his studies in Mathura, Swami Dayanand devoted himself to awakening the masses.

A point has to be specifically noted about his two known biographies (*Pune Text* and *The Theosophist*): both state that he attended the Kumbh Fair in 1855, yet neither mentions his life during 1856-60, which is the ground for raising several doubts. It is amazing how a youthful person with revolutionary thinking remained untouched by a massive, prolonged Uprising, from which even the Narmada region was not immune, where he claimed to have been.

All three of these biographies have been published as a single book titled *Apna Janmacharitra* (Own Biography), edited and commented on by Er. Adityamuni Vanaprastha and Dr. Vedvrit 'Alok'.

So far as '*Agyat-Jeevani*' is concerned, it speaks of several such places that Swami Dayanand has not spoken of in his authentic biographies or otherwise; however, his sermons and books make it seem as if he had visited them. A special point to note about these places is that several of the unmentioned places were directly or indirectly connected to the 1857 Uprising.

As per his authentic biographies, he never went to the region south of the Narmada. Let us compare this statement with his description of the Rameshwaram Temple in the eleventh chapter of *Satyarth Prakash*:

> "As this temple too remains dark even during the day, lamps are lit day and night. When the water stream is released, the lamp's reflection is flashed like lightning in the water, and it is nothing else. The rock neither decreases nor increases, it remains the same as before. Such a trick is played to deceive the poor ignorant people."

Having read this description, do you still think that Swami Dayanand never visited Rameshwaram? He has not admitted to having ever visited Rameshwaram, nor has any scholar who has worked on his biography.

Dayanand spoke to Blavatsky and Olcott on numerous occasions, and several of them were held informally. Through their personal contact, the two knew a great deal about him. Both of them have remarked on him. Madam HP Blavatsky, in her book *The Caves and Jungles of Hindostan*, writes:

> "From the first day of his appearance Dayanand Saraswati produced an immense impression and got the surname of the 'Luther of India'. Wandering from one town to another, today in the south, tomorrow in the north, and transporting himself from one end of the country to the other with incredible quickness, he has visited every part of India, from Cape Camorin to the Himalayas, and from Calcutta to Bombay."

Colonel HS Olcott writes in the December 1883 issue of *The Theosophist* thus:

> "There are few towns and but one province we believe namely, Madras that Pandit Dayanand did not visit in furtherance of his missionary work, and fewer still where he has not left the impress of his remarkable mind behind him."

There are numerous examples from his books and speeches that reveal his revolutionary mind.

On November 1, 1858, Queen Victoria issued a proclamation, published by the Governor General at Allahabad, stating that the British government had taken over the territories of India from the East India Company and had assumed the Government. She further declared that there will be 'no extension' of the territorial possessions and promised:

> "Firmly relying Ourselves on the truth of Christianity, and acknowledging with gratitude the Solace of Religion, We disclaim alike the Right and the Desire to impose our Convictions on any of Our Subjects."

Promising equal protection of the law and paying due regard to the native customs and traditions, she proclaimed general amnesty with certain conditions which, in fact, nullified the effect of the clemency, as thus:

> "Our Clemency will be extended to all Offenders, save and except those who have been, or shall be, convicted of having directly taken part in the Murder of British Subjects. With regard to such, the Demands of Justice forbid the exercise of mercy. To those who have willingly given asylum to Murderers, knowing them to be such, or who may have acted as leaders or instigators in Revolt, their lives alone can be guaranteed; but in apportioning the

> Penalty due to such Persons, full consideration will be given to the circumstances under which they have been induced to throw off their allegiance; and large indulgence will be shewn to those whose Crimes may appear to have originated in too credulous acceptance of false reports circulated by designing Men."

Many people thought that the proclamation intended to give equal rights, so they praised it. However, the Indian leaders, including Swami Dayanand, saw through its real intention and, putting it in the right context, said that this did not give any amnesty at all. In the eighth chapter of his masterpiece, *Satyarth Prakash*, he writes:

> "Let alone how other countries have come to rule over us due to our ill luck, indolence and negligence, as well as mutual conflict, the fact remains that there is no united, free and fearless state of the Aryans in the country. Whatever remains is being trampled by the invaders. Only a few rulers are free. When evil days dawn, the countrymen have to suffer variously. Howsoever someone else might do, but a native rule is the best kind. Though a foreign government can be perfectly free from religious prejudices, can be impartial towards both natives and foreigners, can be kind, just and beneficent to the natives like their parents, yet having alien rulers can never be fully beneficial."

Thus, it was Swami Dayanand who accorded more importance to Swaraj or self-rule causing extreme suffering even if the alien government was more beneficent. By his experience, however, he was well aware that diversity often impedes unity, so he adds to the above statement:

> "It is extremely difficult to do away with the differences in language, education, customs and traditions; however,

> without doing this, the people can never fully effect mutual good and accomplish their object. So, it is incumbent upon gentlemen to approve of the system as is mentioned in the Vedas, scriptures and ancient history."

This was the reason that he accorded the highest priority to abiding by the Vedas. How he wished to unite the countrymen and strengthen them against the alien government, in support of this can be presented three extracts from his texts, which are all from his masterwork *Satyarth Prakash*:

> "The causes of foreign rule in India are evil habits like mutual disunity, difference of opinion, want of purity in life, absence of learning and teaching, child marriage, indulgence, evil qualities like falsehood etc. It is only when brothers quarrel that an outsider takes advantage of it to become the arbiter."
>
> "It was by mutual disunity that the Kauravas, the Pandavas and the Yadavas were destroyed, yet we are still clinging to the same ailment. Only God knows if the Aryans would ever emancipate themselves from this terrible monster or would drown them all in the ocean of suffering deprived of all pleasures. The Aryans are still following the example of the evil Duryodhana who destroyed his clan, and country, only to multiply their sufferings."
>
> "Ever since the alien flesh-eaters and cow-slaughterers have come to rule over us, we Aryans have been suffering increasingly; because if the source/root is destroyed, there can be no fruit or flower."

Swami Dayanand not only stresses the importance of countrymen being united but also urges them to fight if needed. In his book *Sanskritvakyaprabodhah*, he advises the rulers to discuss war at such critical times. He is also aware of how important strategy, supplies and resources are in a battle, so he states:

> "And with the sinner, one must fight…he is the one who makes the subjects suffer by his injustice, that makes him a bigger sinner…if this be the case, then a large fighting army should be sent duly equipped with all kinds of weaponry, treasure and supplies etc."

Discussing this topic further, he, in the sixth chapter of the *Satyarth Prakash*, describes in detail the manner and strategy of fighting a war. He discusses the importance of spies, the need for training, strategy, and tactics in skirmishes, types and methods of weaponry, different strategies for different types of terrain, and the importance of troops' mental fitness. The examples he cites make it amply clear that they did not belong only to the Vedas or other Vedic literature, but also belonged to the prevailing times in which he lived. In this connection, two interesting instances can be quoted:

> "When you have a smaller force to fight with a larger force, the men should fight in close formation and, if the occasion demands, they should be spread out. When a battle has to be fought moving into an enemy town, fort or army, you should arrange your men in an echelon array or a broad file, fighting much like a two-sided dagger cutting from both sides, and doing this advance into the enemy territory. The army should be garrisoned in diverse types of arrays. If the force is confronted with artillery or musketry fire, the array should form like a serpent, that is, the troops should crawl till they get near the guns, and then the enemy should be attacked or captured and their guns should be turned towards the enemy, using their guns to cause havoc right upon them."
>
> "If you have to fight on a level ground, chariots, horses and

> footmen should be used; and warfare in the sea should make use of the boats; and in shallow water, elephants should be used. Bow-arrows should be used in forests and bushes, while sandy ground is fit for fighting with swords and shields."

Dayanand also remarks on other aspects of warfare, such as motivating the troops, monitoring their skill and loyalty, and providing them with medicines, rations, and other aids. He advises not to fight without an array. He also speaks of the enemy's siege. He advises that it should be surrounded, and that their fodder, grains, water, and fuel should be destroyed or polluted to vanquish the enemy completely. He does not stop at this. Thinking ahead of his time, he also speaks of air warfare using aeroplanes. He also speaks of the importance of spies. He attaches importance to the honour of the vanquished people. He clearly states that the prisoners and captured rulers should be treated well and respectfully:

> "Never indulge in anything mean which does not look after the welfare of the defeated ruler. If he is taken prisoner, his honour should be preserved, so that he can stay there joyfully without any grief. . .Don't taunt him, or mock him. Never bluster before him that you have defeated him, rather he should be respected telling him that 'you are like our brother' etc."

It is worth noting that Dayanand wrote the above statements on the basis of the *Manusmriti*, but the impact of the battles fought in 1857-59 is clearly evident in his writings, which also suggest that he witnessed the battles of the great Uprising from close quarters. The other battles fought in India during his youth included the Anglo-Sikh wars of 1845-46, but at that time he had not yet abandoned his home. After the 1857 Uprising, no more battles were fought in India during his lifetime. Had he been staying in the deep jungles along the Narmada, he would not have modified his statements in the contemporary contexts. He has spoken of the rights of the prisoners of war; in this connection, it would be adequate to mention that the English had not taken even a single prisoner during the numerous battles; whoever they caught, they killed them violently by fire, by hanging, by shooting or by exploding at the cannon's mouth. The statement in this context had certainly come from his experience that war prisoners should be given certain rights.

In his Pune sermons (fifth sermon), he clearly refers to 1857 Uprising in these words:

> "When skirmishes broke out in the year of 1857, it is believed that a European burnt down the large library of Amritrao Peshwa. Just think of the extent of wisdom that was destroyed by this act."

This information, which is not mentioned elsewhere, clearly indicates his active participation in the 1857 Uprising.

Dayanand not only played an active role in it, but also motivated the countrymen to rise against foreign atrocities and rule. In the eleventh chapter of the *Satyarth Prakash*, he refers to the powerful invaders being inflicted with several demerits like favouritism, egotism and injustice, and then he goes on to say:

> "When these demerits are caused, their mutual opposition leads to the rise of a competent person who is able to defeat them; as rose Shivaji and Govind Singh ji to cause destruction of the Muslim rule."

He, in the same chapter, chides his countrymen against imitating the English in these words:

> "They [Englishmen] permit their country's shoe in the office and court, but so is not the case with this native shoe. This should be sufficient to realise how exalted prestige

> they attach to their country's shoes, and little care for the native people. The Europeans have been in the country for a few hundred years, but they continue to adorn their thick clothes as they wore in their country, but they did not abandon their customs and traditions, while many of you have imitated them. From just this, you are proved stupid and they, intelligent. . .This would be proper for you and we serve by body, mind and money for the advancement of all those native substances from which our body is made, is preserved and will continue to be so."

In his text, *Aryavibhivinayah*, he prays:

> "May no alien ruler ever rule us, nor may we ever be enslaved."

In addition to the above, when we carefully examine some additional facts, Dayanand's role in the 1857 Uprising begins to emerge clearly. Prior to this Uprising, the sepoys had risen at several places, such uprisings had occurred in 1857 too. All sepoys did not take part in any one of these places. Secondly, the civilians played no role in eruption anywhere other than at Meerut. This entails that there existed some preplanning which kept all sepoys and civilians in close regular contact.

Acharya Deepankar, in his book *Swadhinata Andolan aur Meerut*, explains that several teams of saints and hermits travelled from village to village to sow the seeds of revolution. A similar kind of description has been made by Savarkar in his book *1857 Ka Swatantrya Samar* (War for Freedom of 1857). In the preceding pages, we have already referred to several points which all point to some preplanning.

No wonder that it was due to this network that the news of punishing the sepoys on May 9 had spread through the entire region quickly. The other places where the troops fought asked for salary or money, and at times, they betrayed the cause just for money or some other privilege, but it was due to Dayanand's inspiration that Meerut emerged as the only place where the sepoys assented to rise even when they were assured of no monetary gain; not only this, when Bahadur Shah Zafar told them that he had no money to pay their salary, the sepoys assured him that they would plunder the English and fill his coffers.

This type of elevated, sublime inspiration can come from an amazing personality, and there seemed to be no other matching personality on the Indian horizon then. Dayanand's organisational skills are amply demonstrated by the fact that he established the Arya Samaj, which continues to flourish even 150 years after his death. In the succeeding analysis, we will examine whether there is any possibility that another person was the Aughar Baba who functioned from the Kali Paltan Temple at Meerut. We have already mentioned that Dayanand himself did not believe the Uprising would succeed in its mission; he thought it could not succeed unless all native rulers and people came together. When he, however, was impressed upon by his Guru, he left no stone unturned to accomplish the task. Had all native rulers and citizens come together, there is every possibility that the country could have been freed from the English shackles as early as 1857, for it was on the strength of the native troops and rulers that the English ultimately succeeded in crushing the revolt cruelly.

Dayanand's connection with Meerut can be gauged from several additional facts as well. When he established the Arya Samaj in 1875, its branches soon spread across all districts of the Meerut Commissionerate. This is most probably due to the contacts he had here from previous times. This is worth noting: between 1857 and 1875, that is, between the Uprising and the establishment of the Arya Samaj, he visited it only once, in 1867, when he did not seem to have been involved in any significant activity. Aryamuni Vanprastha and other scholars agree that he was not a well-known personality until then, and he stayed there for less than two weeks.

Yet another fact demands attention. It was on August 16, 1880 that Swami Dayanand established a trust named the Paropakarini Sabha at Meerut and got it registered the same day, which he later shifted to Ajmer just prior to his death in 1883. The purpose of this trust was to look after his books and property, publish books, and propagate Vedic wisdom and ethics. In the list of trustees, just after the names of Rajas and Maharajas, the fourth name was that of Lala Ramsharandas of Meerut, who was then the vice-president of the Meerut branch of Arya Samaj. About this time, Meerut was a centre of Communists and Marxists, as became evident later. In such a case, having the name of a communist like Shyamji Krishna Verma among the trustees only confirms that, while Dayanand had influenced Meerut, in turn, the land of revolution had impressed Dayanand deeply.

Why Only Dayanand?

A moot point arises: Why is our protagonist none other than Swami Dayanand? Is there no possibility that some other prominent person of the time played this role? In the list below, we have considered a number of people in their youth who were above 20 years of age in 1857, who were capable of achieving the extraordinary feat that the Sanyasi accomplished, and who later earned a name in service to the nation in one or the other field. Different descriptions indicate that the Sanyasi was about 30 years old.

Taking a cue from several books, including *Apna Charitra*, we go on to expand the list of likely people to have played the role of the Hindu Faqir and append our remarks for each.

Prasanna Kumar Tagore (1801-86) was about 56 years old and does not appear to be the youthful Hindu Faqir described in different sources. Moreover, he joined the East India Company in 1854 as an assistant clerk. He had taken part in Raja Rammohan Roy's Sati campaign and was one of the original trustees of the Brahmo Samaj.

Radhanath Sikdar (1813-70) was a mathematician, and he calculated the height of Mount Everest, on the basis of which he was taken into the Company's service in 1851 and retired in 1862. Around 1857, he was busy calculating the height of the Darjeeling hills. His name came into consideration because in 1843 he vehemently protested against the unlawful exploitation of the survey department by Magistrate Vensittart, which was reported in detail in *The Bengal Spectator*, edited by Ramgopal Ghosh. In 1854, he started a Bengali journal called *Masik Patrika* and wrote articles for women's education and empowerment with his Derozian friend Peary Chand Mitra.

Sir Syed Ahmad Khan (1817-98) was a reformer, philosopher and educationist, and is credited as the father of the two-nation theory, which formed the basis of the Pakistan movement. He entered the Company's service in 1838 and rose to be a judge in 1867. During the Uprising, he stuck to his loyalty to the British Raj and was noted for his actions in saving European lives. Of course, he wrote a booklet, *The Causes of the Indian Mutiny*, holding various British policies responsible for the insurrection.

Debendranath Tagore (1817-1905) was a philosopher and religious reformer who joined the Brahmo Samaj in 1842 and, in 1848, founded the Brahmo faith. He undertook political work briefly but generally lacked a revolutionary spirit. The well-known litterateur Rabindranath Tagore was his son.

Ishwar Chandra Vidyasagar (1820-91) was a prominent educationist, writer, translator and social reformer. He made significant efforts to simplify and modify the Bengali prose. He worked for the uplift of women. He worked for the widows' remarriage and against child marriage. It was due to his campaign that the Hindu Widows' Remarriage Act of 1856 was passed, and his efforts led to the Age of Consent Act of 1891, which specified the age of consummation at 12 years. Despite his immense social work, he was not inclined to an armed struggle. During the 1857 Uprising, he was busy managing his newly established Barisa High School.

Peary Charan Sarkar (1823-75) was an educationist and worked for girls' education. He also wrote textbooks, which introduced the English language to the young people, and went on to be translated into almost all major Indian languages. He was the headmaster of Hare School during the Uprising.

Michael Madhusudan Dutt (1824-73) was a Bengali poet and playwright, who converted to Christianity in 1843, which by itself confirms his lack of any work against the Company Raj. About 1857 he was working as the chief interpreter in the court.

Dadabhai Naoroji (1825-1917), also known as the Grand Old Man of India, was a Parsi scholar, educationist and merchant. He moved to London in 1855.

Rajnarayan Bose (1826-1900) was an educationist and writer, and possessed a revolutionary spirit, as he founded the Brahmo Samaj and inaugurated the Hindu Mela, an organisation created to spread nationalist feelings among Indians. He was also a political worker, but he mainly focused on education. He was the grandfather of the eminent revolutionary and philosopher Sri Aurobindo. About 1857, he worked as the headteacher in a school.

Deenbandhu Mitra (1829-73) was a dramatist and educationist. Appointed as the postmaster at Patna in 1857, he continued to work in the post and telegraph department at various places until 1871. He is better known for his play *Neel Darpan*, which brought to the fore the plight of indigo farmers and may have led to the Indigo Revolt in 1858.

Taraknath Palit (1831-1914) was a well-known lawyer and philanthropist. He was associated with the Swadeshi Movement to protest against the partition of Bengal. He was one of the key figures behind the establishment of Ballygunge Science College. During the 1857 Uprising, he was studying in England, from which he returned in 1871 to establish his legal practice.

Premchand Roychand (1832-1906) was a businessman known as the Cotton King and Bullion King. He was a founding member of The Native Share and Stock Brokers Association, today better known as the Bombay Stock Exchange. He does not seem to have participated in the Uprising, as he was busy expanding his business at this time. He also worked for the uplift of education.

Dr Mahendralal Sarkar (1833-1904) was a medical doctor who studied medicine at Calcutta Medical College during the Uprising period; he passed his final examination in medicine with the highest honours in 1860. He later cultivated revolutionary ideas in 1867, but they remained limited to specific areas of science.

Bankimchandra Chatterjee (1838-94) was a novelist, poet, essayist and journalist. He wrote Vande Mataram, the national song, in his Bengali masterpiece *Anandmath*. In 1857, he was yet below twenty and studying, while his father served with the East India Company.

Upon exploring the lives and activities of the above-named personalities and others, we believe our research should remain focused on Swami Dayanand. This is, of course, true that direct evidence is absent; however, there exist numerous indirect and circumstantial proofs, which we have discussed in the preceding pages.

Dayanand has played a vital role in shaping the country's present form. Among those inspired by him have been several great freedom fighters who made a supreme sacrifice. Some of the people he influenced immensely include Shyamji Krishna Varma, Subhash Chandra Bose, Lala Lajpat Rai, Madam Cama, Vinayak Damodar Savarkar, Lala Hardayal, Madanlal Dhingra, Ram Prasad Bismil, Mahadev Govind Ranade, Swami Shraddhanand, and many others. He has been admired by many great people, including Swami Vivekananda, Ramakrishna, Bipin Chandra Pal, Sardar Vallabhbhai Patel, Shyama Prasad Mukherjee, Romain Rolland, and others. This list also enunciates the type of revolutionary thought he possessed. Despite his rigid demeanour, he influenced everyone who came into contact. No wonder it was he, and none else, who excited the sepoys at Meerut to realise the task assigned to him and ultimately succeeded in his goal.

16: After Delhi

You have already read how things started to unfold in and around the Red Fort after the revolutionary sepoys marched to Delhi. Overcoming the initial hurdles, when the sepoys approached Bahadur Shah Zafar, they looked for the young Sanyasi who had led them there; however, they were unable to trace him anywhere around; he seemed to have disappeared like a shadow in bright light.

Dayanand had accomplished the task assigned to him in letter and spirit. He was bound to follow the instructions his Guru had given; one of them was to keep his identity secret. He had inspired the Sepoys and taken over the reins of command, though only for a brief period of one night, which was the most critical time in the Uprising's history. As per his Guru's instructions, with its eruption, his task was as good as accomplished. It was now more of a political-military affair, and this was beyond what he was supposed to do. It was the proper time to proceed towards accomplishing his higher goal! No one noticed whether he had entered the fort gate or had just moved away from outside. Amidst the prevailing confusion, the sepoys were all focused on the unfolding events, with a likely skirmish with the native regiment garrisoned there. He realised that it was the most opportune moment to move away unnoticed to work towards his higher, nobler goal.

Tall and sturdy, Dayanand stole a panoramic view of what was unfolding before his bright eyes, chanted a holy verse with his right hand raised in the benediction mode as if wishing the revolutionaries good luck, and then strode away along the moat and gradually moved away from the Red Fort. Soon, he was treading the road towards the south. His Guru had specifically asked him to keep his identity under wraps. To do his bidding, he had decided to take refuge in the jungles along the Narmada, where he had been once before, as he knew that his secrecy would remain intact there. The dense jungles would help him remain shrouded in mysterious incognizance for as long as he wished.

In the past decade, he had undertaken a number of long foot marches, and this was one of them. On the way, he passed by Mathura, but he had no plans to seek his Guru's blessings at this hour; he walked approximately 800 kilometres over the next month and made sure that his identity remained a secret. He stayed only at small temples in villages or treetops for the night, and interacted little with the people he met. He never spoke of his role in the Uprising or his mission at Meerut or Delhi. He has maintained absolute silence for an unknown period of about three years of his life. He has described in his biography what happened when he approached the Narmada bank, which you have already read in the preceding pages. He would wait here for the Uprising to subside, which would continue to burn brightly over the next two years. It was from here that he would return to his Guru in 1860, after the Company Raj ended and the British crown took over the reins of the country. From then on, the study under the teacher would help him gain glory in the coming years.

What disappoints a curious reader the most is that he has not described his contribution to the great Uprising and ended his biography abruptly, though he has left some indications in his sermons and books towards it. He had done this on purpose, as he was obliged to keep his identity a secret, because any trace of his role in it would have attracted severe reaction from the English, which would have nipped in the bud his higher goal. We would have lost a great leader who went on to transform the nation.

17: A Brief Life Sketch

A careful study of the life of Swami Dayanand reveals a specific character trait: he did not accept any pre-established fact easily, and once he had made up his mind, he would stick to it. It was revolutionary thinking that would aid him not only in sparking the 1857 Uprising but also in defining Hinduism in a new way. Certain experiences in his childhood and youth profoundly influenced and shaped his thought.

Dayanand was born on February 12, 1824, in the village of Tankara, in Morvi state, in present-day Gujarat. There are diverse opinions about his date of birth, yet most of the scholars agree on this date. His father, Karshanji Tiwari, called his first son Moolji. He was a devotee of Lord Shankar, so he also called his son Moolshankar. Other family members addressed him as Dayalji. He belonged to a respectable and wealthy family with zamindari rights. He conducted Moolji's education at home, which included studying grammar and religious scriptures, in addition to the *Yajurveda-Samhita*.

With his profound belief in the faith, Karshanji wished that his son would follow the Shaiv faith, which worships Lord Shiva. Moolshankar was 14 years old when he came across a life-changing spectacle. It was the festival of Shivratri. Karshanji explained to him the importance of this holy day and the fasting observed on this occasion. He got him ready to pray and meditate to Lord Shiva, sitting up awake all night in the temple's sanctum. All devotees sat down near the Shivlinga and prayed. Late into the night, they all started to doze, but the young Moolshankar prayed in a fully conscious state, wishing to be blessed with the divine grace of Shiva. As all dozed, mice ran out of their holes and started to partake of the offerings on the Shivlinga. Looking at this, the adolescent sank into deep thought, and his belief in idol worship began to shake. Without completing his prayers, he stood up; not only this, he broke his fast too, for which he had to face his father's wrath. In addition, refusing to listen to the logic behind idol worship, he had determined something else in his mind.

In the coming years, Moolji lost his sister and uncle. Separation from the loving people left him detached; he now thought about freeing himself from domestic bonds. As such, the thoughts overpowered his mind; he discussed them with his friends; however, this leaked to his family members. Looking at his inclination towards detachment, they determined to marry him to a suitable girl. At this, Moolji protested, saying he wished to study further at Kashi.

This was not approved, but his father agreed that he could study with a scholar who lived in an adjacent village. All this while, Moolji was growing more certain in his views on detachment inclining towards asceticism. He happened to express these sentiments once again. When his family members learned of this, they not only summoned him back but also began making preparations for his wedding.

By this time, Moolji was 21 years old, and the year was 1846. Past midnight one day, when all family members were deep in slumber, he abandoned the house. As he negotiated with the paved and unpaved pathways in the night, he crossed Tankara before taking a brief rest. The following day, he walked all day and at sunset, stopped at a Hanuman Temple in a desolate place. He belonged to a wealthy family, so he had a few rings and some money on hand. As he trod on the unknown tracks, he came across some recluses, who grabbed these 'worldly possessions' in the name of '*Moh*' or attachment, saying that he could never attain asceticism with them.

As he moved further, he was initiated into Naishthik Brahmacharya at Sayla on the recommendation of a Brahmachari. With this, he adorned saffron silk clothes and *toomba* (*kamandal* or ewer). Thus, he proceeded on the path of Yoga and meditation. Now, he was on the lookout for a scholarly Yogi who could teach him. On the way, some ascetics mocked him for his silken clothes; he abandoned them, too, and now wore a cotton dhoti. He heard of the fair at Siddhapur to be held in the month of Kartik, and he headed towards it, hoping to find a scholar there for further guidance. It was on his way there that an acquaintance spotted him, and this was how his family learned of his whereabouts. At Siddhapur, he stayed at Neelkanth Mahadev Temple, where his father found him. He first chided him for his vagabond conduct and forced him to change his garb. He also posted some policemen to keep an eye on him. On the other hand, Moolji was resolved to discover the truth and attain wisdom, so he slipped through the dozing policemen and hid in the tower of a temple. The policemen came looking for him, but without success.

The next day, he commenced his journey from there. Taking the route via Ahmedabad, he arrived in Baroda, where he met Brahmanand Brahmachari; the two discussed Vedanta. Now he wished to study earnestly. He noticed that cooking and begging for food took up a lot of time, so he decided to embrace Sanyas, or hermitage. At Chanod, he met Swami Purnanand Saraswati and expressed his desire. At first, the Swami tried to avoid him; however, when he found Moolji fully resolute, he initiated him into Sanyas. This was how the energetic youth emerged in the incarnation of Swami Dayanand Saraswati; he was the person destined not only to be the inspirer of one of the greatest revolutions in the world, but also the founder of Vedanta through the transformation of the world's psyche.

In his new avatar, Dayanand spent most of his time in Yoga, meditation and study. The more wisdom he acquired, the more curious he felt. He would head to any place where he felt he could find wisdom. He would contact any scholar, saint or hermit who could help him attain virtue. This was how he kept wandering from place to place in search of an able Guru.

This was under this endeavour that he arrived at Haridwar on the occasion of Kumbh Fair in 1855. Conclaves of the saints and the wise were and are a regular feature of the Kumbh. Swami Dayanand must have greatly benefited from them. Owing to his wide travels and discussions with scores of knowledgeable scholars, his wisdom had turned unique and transparent. Whomever he talked to, he would cast his spell on him. With this, he earned some fame, yet he continued to consider himself a student and kept himself fully engaged in the search for wisdom until his thirst was fully satiated. We have already narrated to you this entire episode of how he came to be involved in the 1857 Uprising. He not only became involved in it but also ensured it would go on to shake the very foundations of the Company government.

Even before he took up the reins of the great Uprising, he knew that not all the factors were in place that could help it succeed, yet he did all that was necessary to bring it about. Having accomplished the mission he was assigned, he entered a period of anonymity and returned to Swami Virajanand in 1860. This time, he was destined to earn what he had abandoned his house for. He erased from his memory all previous un-Vedic knowledge he had earned. After the Uprising, the country faced a severe crisis and an acute deficiency of food grains. This had an adverse impact on him, too, and he had to survive on eating just grams. Despite all the difficulties he faced, he did not abandon his goal. Some merciful people came to his aid, providing him with facilities for his stay, lighting, and books.

The Sanyas, together with the perfection of intellect, the brightness of perseverance, and the scholarliness of the Guru, helped Dayanand advance toward his goal continuously. Virajanand was a strict teacher; he did not like repeating his lessons. This was the reason many of his pupils dropped out; however, Dayanand was a motivated disciple; he was ready to endure any hardship to achieve what he desired, and this ultimately led to his success. Virajanand himself said to him, "Dayanand, many a pupil came to and went from this cottage, but the joy I felt in teaching you was unique; your logic is impeccable and appreciable. There is every possibility that you will negate all false doctrines."

Dayanand was with Virajanand for 2.5 years. When it was time for Gurudakshina, or the payment of fee to the teacher, he had nothing but a few cloves. At this, the learned Guru said, "The country is drowned in the darkness of ignorance. Trapped in false beliefs and evil rituals, people feel as if they are living in hell. The roots of superstition are growing deeper. The teaching-learning and contemplation-meditation over Vedic scriptures have evaporated. Various doctrines and beliefs have taken hold, pushing society towards its evil consequences. Go save society from this unfortunate fate. Devote yourself fully to the well-being of the world. Shake awake the dormant countrymen. This work will count towards my *Gurudakshina*."

To abide by the Guru's bidding, Dayanand devoted himself fully. From then on, he travelled from town to town, met people, challenged orthodox practices, guided people to the virtuous path, and thus continued accomplishing his goal. Gradually, the number of people impressed by him increased. He not only contacted the common masses but also debated with scholars, thereby helping spread true knowledge. He came into contact with several rulers and princes, and he did his best to show the true path. All people bowed before his scholarly learning and logic. He awakened people to the prevailing evil practices; at the same time, he deeply exposed the illogical and evil practices in other faiths. He liked to call a spade a spade, even if it hurt someone's sentiments. His harsh dialogues also augmented the number of his enemies. He studied the Vedas to explain other ancient texts, developing a profound knowledge of Hinduism that helped him sift the chaff from the grain.

Dayanand was a man of irrepressible fortitude. Once in Ajmer, in the presence of the then ruler, he began to enumerate the demerits of the Vallabh faith, that the ruler followed. Growing angry, the ruler asked his followers to disrupt the assembly. Dayanand, without getting restless, challenged him and said, "I know well how to debate on scriptures, as I know how to wield arms." This forced his adversaries to quit immediately.

To propagate his mission, he participated in the Kumbh Fair twice more. We have told you that he participated in it for the first time in 1855, from which he was inclined to take to revolutionary thought. During his campaigns, he struck hard at malpractices. He allowed the women the right to recite the Gayantri Mantra, and also opposed untouchability.

Once at Karnavas during the Ganga Fair, a wealthy person of Karoli, Rao Karnasingh, organised the Raslila (a dramatic depiction of Krishna and His women followers), and also invited Dayanand, who refused to attend. At this, Karnasingh approached him to express his displeasure, but Dayanand termed the Raslila as an embarrassing act. Growing furious at this, Karnasingh unsheathed his sword. In a flash, Dayanand clutched his wrist and grabbed the sword, breaking it into two. On another occasion, too, Karnasingh dared to kill Dayanand, but his evil plan was divulged just in time.

With time, Dayanand became renowned for his logic and scholarly learning. He was incomparable at making his point humorously. Once, at Kasganj, a scholar debated with him. He seated himself on the high altar of the temple. When it was brought to his notice that it was no good etiquette to occupy a higher place than the ascetics, he retorted that he was a scholar and could not occupy a lower seat. At this, Dayanand remarked, "Well, let him be seated there. Occupying a higher seat does not make a person a scholar, and if this could be the case, the crow on the tree branch there would certainly be more learned than he." Listening to this, the scholar felt humiliated.

As Dayanand's fame spread and his views became popular, plans were afoot to murder him. He was aware that the number of his enemies was rising, so he started to give a concrete shape to his views in the form of books. By 1875, he had written several books, including *Satyarth Prakash*, *Vallabhacharyamata-khandan*, *Swami Narayanamata-khandan*, *Vedantaghvanta-nivarana*, and others. It was in Bombay (now Mumbai) that he first called the Satsang or assembly held there the Arya Samaj, so that the Satsang could continue and his views could spread there even in his absence. The same year, he established the Arya Samaj. He explained its rules and other relevant aspects, which he later abridged when the Arya Samaj was established at Lahore.

In 1875, Dayanand stayed in Pune, where Mahadev Ranade organised his sermons. He delivered a total of 15 lectures; it was in the last of these that he narrated his biography, on the reporting of which it was published in the newspapers then. The existence of this biography is recognised, but it is not considered fully authentic or credible because it was published based on media reporting, so it is considered deficient in terms of trust and credibility.

At times, Dayanand was told not to use harsh terminology about other religions and faiths; however, he was never impressed by how happy or angry others felt. He always spoke what appeared right and true to him. He said that he often wanted to review rather than criticise. He compared his harsh talks with the purgative medicine that can cause vomiting and nausea, yet makes one feel good after the germs have been removed from the body. It remains true that even his opponents found themselves compelled to approve several of his arguments as they were based on logic and reasoning.

During the final period of his life, he also established the Paropkarini Sabha, and all the wealth he earned from the sale of his books, etc., was entrusted to this trust. He nominated Rana Sajjansingh, the ruler of Udaipur, as its chairman.

When Maharaja Yashwantsingh of Jodhpur invited Dayanand, he was advised against accepting the invitation. He, however, accepted the invitation. He was so advised because the ruler was indulging in prostitution. Everybody knew that Dayanand was a person who could not be restrained from remarking on such evil conduct, which could lead to trouble; this eventually happened. The ruler was fully drowned in the fascination of a prostitute named Nanhijaan. When Dayanand pointed out this misconduct to the ruler, the ruler began to distance himself from her, which she could not tolerate. Using her resources, she allegedly served him arsenic in complicity with the cook Dhaulamishra. This occurred on September 29, 1883. His condition deteriorated day by day. He was first taken to Mount Abu for treatment, and then to Ajmer. It was here on October 30, 1883, that he bid farewell to this mortal body forever.

Dayanand has several accomplishments to his name; we are all aware of the establishment of the Arya Samaj, his social service activities, and his books; however, his role in the 1857 Uprising remained eclipsed from public view for a long time. We have worked earnestly to bring this fact to the public's attention. The fact remains that there is no substantial evidence available on this, and some doubts will persist until concrete evidence emerges. We are determined to work towards it to provide clarity to our presentation.

18: The Outcome

The Uprising had taken place, and there was a need to spread it to the widest possible area. After the sepoys at Meerut rose on May 10, 1857, they marched to Delhi, declared the 87-year-old Bahadur Shah Zafar as their leader on May 11, and occupied Delhi on May 12. Violence continued for five days. Wherever the sepoys seized the Englishmen, common people would come to the field with their domestic weapons. At several places, the citizens rose by themselves, and the sepoys reached there only later. In some places, civilians held their ground, and the revolutionary army never reached them. All people seemed to have risen with a common goal, which was to unite the entire country and to drive the atrocious, barbarous Englishmen out of the country. The English retreated, but not without saying: *Shehenshah-e-Alam, Delhi to Palam*. They were wrong, neither, as the last Mughal emperor was a ruler only in name, having been at the mercy of other powers for several decades.

Appointing Bahadur Shah Zafar as the leader can be termed a mistake, too. Owing to his advancing age and limited resources, he was unable to provide effective leadership to sepoys and citizens. Owing to the incompetent ruler at the helm, even the royal family was prone to secret conspiracies, many of which were hatched by the princes themselves. This led to uncertainty enveloping it. Zafar was unable to provide inspiring leadership while the country was at his beck and call. The Sikhs had a bitter experience at the Mughals' hands, and despite their total defeat against the English just a decade back, they did not support the Uprising;

rather, they came in support of the imperialist Englishmen. The Sikhs had tasted a massive defeat at the hands of the English in these battles. Yet, they believed that the *Purabias* (or people of present-day Eastern Uttar Pradesh and Bihar), forming a major part of the Bengal Army, were responsible for their woes, as it was on their strength that the English were able to occupy the Punjab; and in this Uprising, the *Purabias* were the chief actors. To block the Mughals' rise back to the central power, the Sikhs rendered the English crucial aid in both forms—men and material. The English forces overcame the revolutionary forces through barbaric attacks and plunder. Had the Sikhs not stood by them, their success would have been much tougher, if not impossible.

At that time, the railway was the chief means of transportation, and the telegraph was the only means of communication. Both of them were under English control. As a result, it took a long time for news of the Meerut Uprising to spread to other places.

The way the English were taken by surprise at Meerut, people came to think that they were not unconquerable. It was a proven fact that the chief sources of power for them were the native sepoys, and when they rose, the English had no way out but to retreat. The fact was quite motivating for the masses. Now they were planning to stand up against the English. Power lies in unity; the people firmly believed in this edict. There was a dire need for resources, which were not abundantly available. Any war or revolution could not be sustained for long in the absence of supplies.

While the revolutionary spirit played its part, others were more interested in vested interests. This was the reason that, despite the Uprising occurring in a quite large area, it had yet to embrace the entire nation. There were several people, zamindars and native rulers, who were still cooperating with the English.

In some places, the flame of the revolution was so fierce that everything else seemed to have lost momentum. At others, it gradually lost its gleam. There were places where revolution did not see the light of day.

Having emerged from the initial shock, the English were now busy planning how to suppress the revolutionaries. They had never conjectured that all classes of people would rise against them in so short a span of time. In some places, the Uprising was sporadic; only isolated occurrences were witnessed, as in the Punjab. In several places, including at Amritsar, Ambala and others, mass graves have been found which tell the tale of English barbarity. It appears that the sepoys and other revolutionaries were buried alive there. It would be folly to think that no revolution occurred in the Punjab, but that is not true. It certainly did, but it could not expand, as it failed to take a popular form.

In the provinces where the revolution spread extensively, the English, in their bid to suppress people, shamed even humanity as they committed such cruel, heartless acts which filled the Indians with aversion for them forever.

Delhi had fallen to the revolutionaries, yet there seemed to be no upheaval in other parts of the country. The English, too, had emerged from the initial shock and were now actively planning to bring Delhi back under their control. It was like psychological pressure on them, as it was the centre of the native powers, though the East India Company had yet to make Calcutta its capital.

It was about this time that news of the revolution began to filter in from other parts of the country. By the first week of June, numerous towns across Uttar Pradesh, Bihar, and central India were up in arms. The prominent places where the Uprising erupted included Bareilly, Kanpur, Lucknow, Banaras, several places in Bihar, including Arrah, Jagdishpur, Patna, and also those in the

Rajputana and Madhya Pradesh. What was a relief for the English was that South and Northeast India remained quiet. However, sporadic incidents occurred there as well. West India, aside from Kolhapur, remained calm as well. The English, too, had awakened from their complacent slumber. They would now act proactively and heartlessly whenever they received any sensation of upheaval from anywhere.

Some princely states openly stood by the English, including those of Kashmir, Hyderabad, Bhopal, and others. Nepal too sided with the English. In some places, the Uprising was terrible, as in Kanpur, Lucknow, Delhi, and Bihar, and bringing it under control would require Herculean efforts. In certain places, the masses carried forward the revolution's goal under local leadership, as the sepoys were not available there. Among such places, the Meerut region and its surrounding areas remained prominent. In this region, the revolution erupted in villages, and so many sacrifices were made that remain unaccounted for to date.

Delhi

With the arrival of the Meerut sepoys at Delhi on May 11, 1857, the native regiments welcomed and joined them. The following five days saw a number of skirmishes for complete domination. The English were in for serious trouble, suffering numerous casualties. Common people also cooperated with the sepoys, which added to their woes. As they lost control of the city of Delhi, they camped in the hilly area to the west, called Ridge, and busied themselves with how to occupy it again. It was a strategically important area, as the Yamuna and hills provided them with natural cover. At the same time, they had the advantage of height to bombard at considerable distance. This area also gave them the advantage of easy access to supplies from the north-west, as the Punjab lay in that direction, where the Uprising had not been widespread, and the Sikhs were generally in their favour.

The English launched several attacks to capture Delhi, but to no avail. As the revolution spread to other regions, the strength of native forces here continuously increased. The sepoys often launched sneak attacks and sallies, causing losses in life and property. The English had grown habituated to a luxurious life and abundant amenities. However, now they had to make do with tents. The period of waiting lengthened from minutes to hours, then to days and weeks, while there was little change in the ground situation. The month of August now set in. Being devoid of control over Delhi had staked their prestige as a prominent power in India. Despite being garrisoned in the peripheral areas and facing extreme pressure, they still hoped to get back to Delhi. They could not abandon this area at any cost, as it would entail a complete cut-off from the Punjab, which would shatter their dream of crushing the revolution.

The English availed themselves of opportunities to gather resources and obtain supplies from wherever possible. They not only commissioned forces and supplies from across India, but also sailed their regiments from Europe, where the Crimean War had recently come to an end. When two military columns from Shimla and Meerut joined them, they could feel somewhat relieved. On their march to Delhi, these two columns had committed mindless atrocities on the villages *en route*. Committing plunder and destruction, they did not spare anyone whomsoever they caught. The main part of these columns was composed of the Gorkha troops who had been dispatched on contract by the Nepalese king, as they had little sympathy for the mass revolution.

These columns took on the revolutionary forces at the Badli-Ki-Sarai battle and defeated them. This limited the native forces within the city's precincts around Delhi. However, they still had outlets to Agra and Bareilly, etc., to obtain supplies. With this victory, the English seized it, but the presence of a large number of native troops made them feel as if it was the other way around. Both sides kept undertaking stealthy attacks, causing some damage to the opponents. Though these minor attacks caused little harm, they forced the opponent to keep guard day and night, harming their motivation and training. These sallies can be compared with the terrorist attacks in the present times, in which a few terrorists sneak into an area, attack and flee. However, as a consequence, a large number of troops have to be deployed on precautionary guard duty, which causes havoc with their motivation.

It would be adequate to tell about Bakht Khan, who was a Subedar in the Bengal Army garrisoned at Bareilly. He loved the English lifestyle. He was little interested in the Uprising when he received news about the Meerut eruption. When people urged him to rise, and when he himself saw the barbaric atrocities being committed by the English forces, he decided to rise. He took over the command of the Bareilly native sepoys and marched to Delhi on June 11. On July 2, he was welcomed by Bahadur Shah Zafar, who bestowed on him the title of Sahib-e-Alam, appointing him the commander-in-chief of the native forces. It is also claimed that he brought in much wealth, including four lakh rupees, which earned him this honour. Until now, it had not been possible to pay the native sepoys' salaries, so they were engaged in loot and plunder, causing a decline in civil support for the revolutionary forces. This money helped control the sepoys a great deal.

Bakht Khan also learned that the Mughal princes were involved in plunder in the city, so he issued strict instructions to prevent such incidents. This led to groupism. The princes, on their part, attempted to bring Bakht Khan into submission; however, they could not succeed, as his popularity and army grew. On July 9, he attacked and occupied Tees Hazari, making it his first major victory. Instead of celebrating, some elements tried to sow seeds of division, mainly owing to ego and envy. The bug did not stop at this; conspiracies were being planned to break Hindu-Muslim unity. Despite Bakht Khan's control over the area, English spies might have infiltrated the area who were behind such disunity plots. Taking a cue from what was happening around, he decided to ban cow slaughter on the occasion of Bakreed, which fell in July. He openly declared that any such slaughterer would be considered a traitor to the Mughal ruler and would be eligible for the death penalty.

The problem seemed more acute the following month, when a plan was afoot to attack the English garrison in the hills beyond Alipore, extending to Najafgarh. The attack was to be a pincer manoeuvre by two columns, one under his personal command. The two columns failed to act in accordance with the joint plan, causing a significant loss to the second (Neemach) army, and Bakht Khan had to retreat. Thus, this defeat was a great drawback to the unity of the native forces, which was already fragile. The English forces, on the other hand, were growing stronger by the day.

In the meanwhile, the revolutionary army too tried to strengthen and equip itself. Now the manufacture of the shallow cannons had set off, for which the making of simple balls was also underway. All this while the English were losing confidence in their officers, in view of the commanders falling victim to the enemy's superior tactics. It was then that the Company's Calcutta headquarters dispatched John Nicholson to set things in order. He arrived in Delhi on August 14 in the company of his Sikh, Pakhtoon and European troops. This strengthened the English might considerably. The native forces, too, realised that it would be difficult to take on such a mighty force. Foreseeing their likely defeat not in the distant future, they were ready to even compromise and sue for peace. Now the situation had changed, and the English were no longer interested in a peace pact; they wanted revenge, in all the barbarity that could be unleashed.

From September 7, the English forces opened an onslaught on Delhi, starting with the heavy cannonade, bringing untold misery to the defending revolutionaries and civilian populace. This made the defenders more resolute. When John Nicholson launched the ground attack, he tasted initial success but suffered a massive loss. He had to work hard to keep his foot in the city, while his commander, Wilson, wished to withdraw, despite his junior officers appealing to him to stay put. A week-long battle brought the English into the proximity of the Red Fort, which forced Bahadur Shah Zafar to abandon his dynastical refuge to head to Humayun's Tomb, where he was arrested. Bakht Khan had advised him to accompany him, but he refused. Later, Bahadur Shah was put on a kangaroo court, by which he was held guilty of all accusations and sent to Rangoon (Burma, now Myanmar) where he died in the year 1862 under English captivity in a terrible condition. Two of his princes and a grandson were taken captive on a promise of safety, but were murdered in cold blood. With this, the Mughal dynasty declined forever.

Bakht Khan moved to Awadh, where he had to take part in the Uprising. He took an active part in the battle fought on March 16, 1858, suffering heavy losses of men and cannons. He probably died on May 13, 1859, but several myths prevail about it.

The English had to fight hard for the occupation of each alley and street in Delhi, and suffer a massive loss in life. To take revenge, they unleashed the most terrible atrocities and plunder. The heartlessness with which the common citizens were slaughtered forced the well-known poet Ghalib to say that he found a stream of blood before him and was not sure what more dreadful things he would have to see in the coming days.

Kanpur

Cawnpore, as Kanpur was spelt then, was a flourishing cantonment in the years preceding the 1857 Uprising, with a division headquarters for the native units comprising three infantry (1st, 53rd, and 56th) and one cavalry (2nd) regiments. The commander here was Hugh Wheeler, who had embraced Indian traditions and had even married an Indian woman. He had built his trust and grew popular among the native sepoys. This convinced him that the sepoys would not rise in a rebellion, which was rumoured to erupt on May 31. The news of the Meerut Uprising reached here by the middle of May, after which the native sepoys began sending their families back to their villages.

As the days passed, the English suspected that the final date of the Uprising was May 31, yet Wheeler continued to have a firm belief in the native troops. Moreover, he felt that even if they broke into revolt, they would move to Delhi, as they had done at Meerut and in several other places. So, he conjectured that he needed to make security arrangements to deal with the initial onslaught. To do this, he arranged for a fortified refuge to the south of the town in a large building, surrounded by a boundary, with provisions of arms, ammunition and artillery as well as facilities for the stay of all European men and women. He passed instructions that all men and their families needed to shift to the building in case of an emergency. This decision was strategically wanting, in that he possessed the magazine (artillery centre) to the north of the town, equipped with various amenities. He felt so confident that he dispatched two companies to Lucknow, which was then seized by the revolutionary sepoys. What gave him added confidence was the fact that Nana Saheb, who could prove to be a source of scourge, appeared to be in his favour. When he felt that the sepoys were in the process of rising, he invited none else but him. This was how Nana Saheb entered Kanpur with his force of 300 troops and two cannons, along with ancillary staff and provisions.

On May 30, there was a minor eruption, followed by a revolt along the Ganges at Fatehgarh, near Kanpur, to suppress which Wheeler commissioned a company. In the ensuing conflict, however, three English officers were killed while one of them escaped safely.

Despite the incident at Fatehgarh, the native regiments in Kanpur remained quiet. The Europeans, however, had a shivering spine at the prospect of the likely upheaval, so they moved to the building with the bag and baggage they had prepared for the purpose; not only this, they mounted cannons which the native troops considered a threat to themselves.

On June 2, a minor incident occurred again. An English troop, inebriated to the extreme, fired at a native sepoy. When reported, he was declared not guilty, which cultivated dissatisfaction among the native sepoys. Soon, rumours were the order of the day among them; one of them alarmed them; it said that all native sepoys would be filed in the parade ground and shot dead.

The situation continued to aggravate but largely remained quiet. On June 5, a major incident occurred. The native sepoys belonging to the 2nd Cavalry killed their officer, Risaldar-Major Bhawanisingh, for his loyalty to the *Firangis* or foreign masters. At this time, the other native regiments remained loyal to their employers, yet the sound of firing disturbed their peace of mind. The English, on the other hand, thought that they were now rising in rebellion, so they opened the cannon fire.

All this while, about 150 native sepoys of the 53rd Infantry, posted for the magazine's security, had not risen. When Nana Saheb arrived in the magazine with his men, they rather welcomed him, as they felt he was loyal to the English. But so was not the case. Having entered the premises, he took over the command of the artillery. Then he announced that he was against the English. He gathered the treasury and artillery assets and marched to the Grand Trunk Road. It was at this time that his secretary, Azimulla Khan, advised him that his march to Delhi would mean being subservient to the Mughal ruler. At the same time, he was now in a position to establish his own Maratha empire. Heeding the advice, he decided to capture Kanpur and returned. It was at this juncture that the rebel sepoys joined hands with him.

On June 6, Nana Saheb launched an invasion of the fortified building. It might seem odd that the English did not take seriously the warning that Nana Saheb had conveyed to them in a letter expressing his intention to attack. As a result, an open insurrection broke out, and all native sepoys joined Nana Saheb's forces. Thus, over the next five days, Nana Saheb's strength had soared to about 10,000-15,000 troops.

The English in the building, on the contrary, faced terrible times. There were about 1,000 Europeans, comprising troops, traders, assistants, and family members. Water was deficient, and supplies were irregular. Dysentery and cholera broke out, causing casualties. As if these problems were not enough, Nana Saheb's cannons wreaked havoc on them. The only relief for them was that there had not been a ground attack. By June 21, about one-third of the seized Europeans had lost their lives, while the number of the wounded was by no means small. It was only due to their magazine that Nana Saheb had not launched an effective ground attack. Wheeler was crying hoarse, entreating Lucknow for reinforcements, but those requested were themselves facing a rough time.

It was June 23, the day the battle of Plassey was fought 100 years ago, which ultimately led to imperial rule in India. It was on this day in 1857 that Nana Saheb launched a physical attack; however, his troops could not break into the garrison. Despite this, the English suffered massively due to the combined effects of cannonade and disease. To them, survival seemed difficult, if not impossible. They somehow wanted to get out of the siege, but this could not be done without Nana Saheb's express consent. It was by coincidence that Nana Saheb sent a European prisoner to Wheeler and promised him to help move out towards Allahabad safely. Seeing no other hope, Wheeler assented to this proposal.

A dreaded incident occurred on June 27, spreading bitterness throughout. After Wheeler assented to the proposal for a safe rescue, Nana Saheb arranged forty boats at Sati Chaura Ghat. He made suitable provisions for rations, too. He also provided palanquins, elephants and bullock carts for the Englishmen, their families, the wounded and the sick. Not only this, but they were also allowed to carry small arms.

At 8 in the morning, the caravan arrived at the Ganga bank. The water was shallow at the Ghat, so several boats ran aground, and special efforts were made to launch them. It was an exciting event, for which a large number of people gathered.

Suddenly, a bugle sounded; as if it were a signal, the boatmen jumped from the boats and started swimming towards the bank. Soon, the boats were bombarded, and some caught fire. The Europeans were confounded and started firing with the weapons they had. Soon, a number of native horsemen descended into the water and attacked the European troops in the boats.

Nana Saheb was not present there. When he was informed

of the sudden eruption of violence, he rushed to the spot and explicitly ordered that no woman or child should be harmed, so they all were taken prisoners. Only four English troops could flee from there. Two other English girls are also said to have fled from the scene. Some of them rowed away on a boat, but they were attacked, killing a few of them, while the remaining 12 were captured and brought to Savadaghar, where they were murdered. All other prisoners were taken to Bibighar. One of the four English troops who had fled the place was Captain Thomson. It was he who narrated the occurrence as he perceived in his book *The Story of Cawnpore*. The total number of prisoners brought to Bibighar was about 200 women and children. As many of them suffered from dysentery and cholera, casualties were occurring among them.

Soon, a large English army was sent under the command of General Havelock to occupy Kanpur. Nana Saheb thought he could convince him to stay back in Allahabad in return for the prisoners, but this did not materialise, and the English army kept advancing towards Kanpur. To check its advance, Nana Saheb dispatched his army. The two clashed at Fatehpur on July 12, resulting in Havelock's victory. Another skirmish took place at Awang three days later, but the result was no different.

It was on this day that a heartless massacre took place at Bibighar. All prisoners were killed and thrown into an adjacent well. The historians are not in agreement about who ordered it. It appears that Nana Saheb was not in its favour. Yet, the circumstances unfolded such that he was unable to do anything about the matter. When the English army advanced to seize Kanpur, it engaged in terrible violence and plunder in all villages that fell on its route. It appears that this occurred in retaliation for the Bibighar incident. Violence cannot be a fitting response to violence, as the future would unfold. When the English occupied Kanpur, they wreaked such a demonic havoc of massacre and violence, sparing no one, that it can shake any person to the innermost soul.

It is worth noting that in this encounter, several women, including dancing girls called Tawaifs, also took part. One of them was a legendary fighter named Azizan Bai, who not only took up arms but also served the sepoys with food, money, and entertainment. She was later captured and executed by General Havelock.

This should be pertinent to describe the leaders of this revolution at Kanpur. Tatya Tope launched an attack on Kanpur in November 1857, but it was unsuccessful. After this, he joined Rani Lakshmi Bai of Jhansi. Little is known about Nana Saheb's fate. It is believed that he crossed over to Nepal and died there in 1859. It is also said that he headed southwards, crossed the Narmada, and tried to inspire a revolution there, in which Swami Dayanand too aided him; however, this remains more conjecture than a confirmed account, as there is no direct or circumstantial evidence in its support. The only remote evidence is that Swami Dayanand has admitted to practising Yoga in the region at this time, as you have read in the preceding pages.

Lucknow

Just one year prior to the 1857 Uprising, the English had conspired to accuse the Awadh Nawab of mismanagement to bring the prosperous province under their direct control, pensioning off the Nawab, Wajid Ali Shah, to Calcutta. This engendered discontent among the masses, which was one potent cause that the English had to confront the stiffest opposition here. Numerous places across Awadh rose in armed struggle, and there were witnessed unique instances of courage, valour and tactics by numerically inferior sepoys and civilians that even European writers have admired. These places included not only Lucknow but also Etawa, Fatehgarh, Faizabad, Ambarpur, Kasganj, Mainpuri, Unnao and others. Lucknow's Commissioner, Sir Henry Lawrence, fortified the Residency, mounting cannons into a strong garrison. The native sepoys launched attack after attack, both ground and artillery, yet they failed to break through. They laid siege to the area, and their onslaught rapidly reduced English manpower.

Having occupied Kanpur, Havelock now turned his attention to Lucknow. He reached the Residency, but fate awaited him: he was trapped in the intense siege the revolutionaries had laid; he was now surrounded, along with those he had come to rescue. Later in October, Campbell attacked Lucknow with a very large force. He opened a new front at Alambagh, leaving it under the protection of the 4,000-troop-strong army, and then went to Kanpur to take on Tatya Tope, defeating him. He returned to Lucknow in March 1858, and this time he led an even larger army, which also comprised the Nepalese army. His fierce attack on March 21 scattered the revolutionary troops, though they continued to adopt guerrilla tactics to harass the English forces.

The Uprising at Lucknow was led by Begum Hazrat Mahal, the wife of Nawab Wajid Ali Shah, who did not accompany her exiled husband and stayed back. She put her son on the throne and fought bravely. Her commander, Maulvi Ahmadulla Shah, led his forces and fell fighting. The Begum struggled for long, but when she could find no succour, she fled to Nepal. As the English had done at numerous other places, they massacred scores of people and did not spare even women and children. After each confrontation, they reached a new height of atrocity, cruelty, and plunder as well.

Jhansi

A heroic figure like Rani Lakshmi Bai is born only once in a while. When the news of the Meerut Uprising reached Jhansi, the 12th Native Infantry Regiment occupied the Jhansi Fort, including its treasury and magazine. A few of the surrendered European officers and their families were killed, but the Rani could not be accused of this act. After this, the native sepoys moved away. Until this time, she did not intend to take on the English; she only became the city's administrator. Taking advantage of the upheaval there, the princely states of Orchha and Datia attacked so as to divide the territory between them. The Rani sought English aid, but in response, they held her guilty of the massacre and did not send any reinforcement. At this, she ordered the manufacture of cannons and successfully confronted the invaders in August 1857. Even now, she was not against the English.

All this while, the English were busy suppressing the Uprising elsewhere and paid no attention to Jhansi; so the Rani continued to administer it. With the passage of time, she and her advisors opted for freedom from the British overlordship. Their determination further hardened when they received news of the cruel revenge and retaliation across numerous places. With this resolve, they fortified the Jhansi Fort with large cannons. Finally, when the English force surrounded Jhansi and invaded it on March 21, 1858, the Rani led her troops in a ferocious repulsion. In the meantime, a message was sent to Tatya Tope for aid. He arrived with his 20,000-strong army, but he could not break through the English siege. It was about this time that the English army managed to breach the fort walls in some places, putting the defending forces in jeopardy and forcing the Rani to abandon the fort.

If you ever visit the Jhansi Fort, you must visit and look down a site called Kudan Sthal, from which this warrior, riding a horse with her minor son tied to her back, jumped over the boundary down to an over 30-feet-deep slanting stony cliff covered with thorny bushes, without a second thought about her or her son's personal safety. Her favourite horse, Badal, sacrificed himself to keep his riders safe. The Rani immediately took another horse and rode away. Until recently, she was not against the English, but now that she had risen against them, no obstacle could be high enough to impede her advance.

From here, she headed to Kalpi, where she joined forces with Tatya Tope. They occupied the place and made preparations for its defence. They faced the English force on May 22, in which she was defeated. Yet without losing courage, she now headed to Gwalior. The Scindia ruler at this time was supportive of the English and was by no means as proud as his predecessors. As soon as he heard of the advancing Rani, he fled the fort, so she faced no difficulty in occupying Gwalior. With this, she founded the Maratha state and appointed Nana Saheb as the Peshwa and his brother Rao Saheb as the Subedar.

On June 16, General Rose led a very large force to attack Gwalior and occupied it. It was on the very next day that time seemed to have paused itself to view the spectacle that was to unfold. Rani Lakshmi Bai, wielding a long sword in one hand and the horse's reins in another, with her son tied to her back, came to the battlefield with her troops. Just about 8 miles from Gwalior, she confronted the English. Despite being numerically inferior, she fought on despite her warriors falling to the enemy onslaught. She was wounded herself.

It is believed that when she was about to breathe her last, she said to an old ascetic that the English should not be able to touch her dead body. With this, she laid down her life in the service of her motherland. The ascetic carried her body to a hut and set it on fire for the final rites. The memorial to the Rani stands at this spot near Gwalior, reminding us of her undaunted courage and invincible spirit.

Tatya Tope wandered from place to place, but he was arrested in April 1859. He was hanged, and there also prevail doubts about whether this is true. Whatever the truth, this unflinching warrior has been celebrated even by his adversaries for his tactics and spirit.

Jagdishpur

For those who chose to sacrifice themselves at the altar of the Uprising in 1857, age was no bar. The oldest warrior to take part in active fighting was 81; he was Babu Kunwar Singh, the zamindar of Jagdishpur. He had been planning for insurrection against the English for quite some time, as there exist proofs of his involvement in such a plan almost a decade earlier.

When the native sepoys rose at Danapur (Patna), they needed a leader. In contemporary Bihar, no one could match the competence and resources that Kunwar Singh possessed, so the sepoys headed to him. He too gladly accepted this massive responsibility and immediately rose to the occasion, launching an attack on Arrah and sieging the government house. When a rescue force was sent, he was badly defeated, but the repeated attacks by the English were too fierce, so he had to retreat to Jagdishpur. A terrible battle ensued, after which he was forced to adopt guerrilla tactics. To bring a wide area under his control, he led his troops across western Bihar and Awadh, fighting battle after battle at numerous places and teaching the enemy a lesson in warfare.

Having completed this long march, he headed back to Jagdishpur. When he was crossing over the Ganga in a boat, the English army fired at him. A bomb struck his right hand, wounding it badly. Fatigued by a long march, he knew he could not survive this wound, so he unsheathed his sword and severed his right hand to offer to the gurgling waters of Mother Ganga. He occupied Jagdishpur after a fierce battle. However, the wound and fatigue overpowered him, and this great freedom fighter breathed his last just two days later on April 26, 1858. After him, his younger brother, Amar Singh, continued the struggle for another year.

We have selected only a handful of the numerous places where the Uprising took place. Courage and valour shown in these battles and skirmishes gave the Indians confidence that all was not lost yet. Several lakhs of people sacrificed themselves, yet not more than a handful of them are known; the majority remain unknown to us. In most places, the struggle continued much as at Meerut, so we return to it to conclude this book.

Meerut

Better known as Krantidhara, or the Land of Revolution, Meerut lived up to the expectations of the warriors when it paved the way for the Uprising. Most people think that the sepoys rose on May 10, 1857, and marched off to Delhi, and that after this, the district remained unruffled amid what was occurring across the length and breadth of the country. So is anything but true. The people here kept the flame of revolution alighted and stimulated it with their countless sacrifices. There are numerous villages not only in Meerut but also in modern-day western Uttar Pradesh where the people faced the mighty, well-equipped English forces with their domestic weapons. We can describe a few of them to help understand the prevailing situation. They are only like the tip of the iceberg that can be seen.

You already know that the Uprising erupted when the civilians started it, and then the native sepoys joined it. They did not stay here for more than a few hours as they marched off to Delhi after dusk set in. The civilians continued with their action for another five days. Most of these conflicts were minor, yet some were quite grave, as the market in Sardhana was plundered and government officials were driven away. In Barnawa, people gathered under the leadership of Qalandar Khan and occupied the town; he was declared its ruler. The English were so bewildered by these incidents that General Hewitt imposed martial law throughout the district. To suppress the local people, a native regiment of Sappers was summoned from Roorkee, which arrived here on May 15 by the Ganga Canal. The Commandant of Meerut, Fraser, was afraid that these people could rise in a revolt, so he asked them to deposit their arms in safe custody, which only excited the sepoys, as the first love for a sepoy is his weapon. When Fraser tried to explain to them, one of the sepoys fired at him. In the ensuing heat, a few more Europeans were killed. After this, the sepoys fled the scene. However, the magazine was ordered to open fire on them. Of these fleeing sepoys, about 50 were killed, while there is no idea what happened to the rest; maybe they marched off to Delhi to join their comrades who were stoking the fire of revolution there. After this, all weapons were withdrawn from the remaining native sepoys at Meerut, and they were now engaged in sundry tasks, such as distribution of posts, bricklaying, helping in the mess, etc.

John William Kaye has described this occurrence in these words:

> "An Afghan sepoy fired his piece from behind the Commandant, and Fraser fell, shot through the back. Others fired at Adjutant Mansell, but missed him; and the Native non-commissioned officer who was in attendance on Fraser

> was killed in the affray. Having done this, the mutineers broke and fled, but their victory was short-lived. A troop of the Carabineers and some Horse Artillery guns were let loose upon them. The greater number escaped; but some fifty of the fugitives were overtaken outside cantonments among the sand-hills, and were killed. And so the Sappers and Miners, as a regiment, ceased to exist."

With this, the Uprising by the sepoys had come to an end, but so was not the case with the civilians. As the revolutionary incidents erupted in other places across the country, the European regiments garrisoned at Meerut were despatched off to different places; only a minuscule force was retained here for security purposes. As the days passed, the people were growing restless and aggressive. While the town was generally tranquil, the people in villages opposed paying the land revenue and attacked the government servants who came for this purpose. These were testing times for the English as it was also the time when the revenue had to be collected.

In the meanwhile, the regiments heading to Delhi from the northern region were gathered in Meerut for onward despatch to take part in the offensive at Delhi. This army, with about 1300 troops, comprised both musketeers and magazine. They marched off from Meerut on May 27 and had scarcely reached the Hindan River by the 30th. Surprisingly they had covered such a small distance in four days, when the native sepoys on May 10 had crossed over to Delhi in one night. They, in fact, had not been indolent or inactive during this time. They burned down all the villages that fell on their route. Normally, they would gather the villagers at one place and set fire all around them. If anyone tried to escape, they would shoot him. They did not spare even women and children. It was a type of extreme barbaric atrocity to befall the civilians and defies all description.

The news of this vehement and mindless violence reached Delhi. At this time, another English army was marching down from Ambala, and if it joined the one from Meerut, it would make defending Delhi very difficult. So, the revolutionary army at Delhi decided to confront the army from Meerut on the sandy banks of the Hindan River. This was how the first battle of Meerut occurred on May 30. This revolutionary force was not strong enough to check the enemy; its troops got scattered in all directions and sought refuge in adjoining villages, which were destroyed by the English cannons.

John William Kaye has described the valour displayed by the two warring sides. Writing of the native sepoys, he notes:

> "It taught us that among the mutineers were some brave and desperate men, who were ready to court instant death for the sake of their national cause. Many acts of heroism of this kind brighten up the history of the war, and many more were, doubtless, performed, of which History has no record."

The defeat on the first day did not deter the revolutionary forces. The following day, they returned with reinforcements. They inflicted heavy losses on the English brigade, as the Europeans found it difficult to operate on the hot, sandy surface. The fighters were supported by a sizeable number of civilians from around; however, they together could not decimate the English force. They had to retreat once again, but today, they moved back in a planned manner, carrying their cannons and other resources safely to Delhi.

To support the revolutionary army at the Hindan bank, Shahmal, the Jat leader of the village Bijrol in the tehsil of Baraut, also came. As soon as he came to know of the Meerut Uprising, he determined to rise too. He was not content with mere non-payment of revenue; he wanted a complete revolution. We have told you that he was present at the secret meeting in Mathura.

He formed a farmer army and attacked the tehsil headquarters. He did not succeed, yet he was able to plunder the treasury. He followed this up with an attack on the police post, which earned him a few muskets too; until now, the men relied only on domestic weapons like swords, lances and sticks. Within a week, he was able to found his state over 84 villages. To expand the revolution, he sent his emissary to the Delhi emperor, who appointed him the subedar of the area north of the Hindan. He supplied grains to the revolutionary army and set up his headquarters at the irrigation department in Baraut. Despite the growing size of his army, he knew he could not take on the English in a direct confrontation, so he adopted guerrilla tactics. In the first week of July, he also fought a face-to-face battle, causing losses to the opponent.

This was how the Khaki Risala was sent after him. Let us know what it was. To suppress the rebellious masses, the English officers at Meerut undertook an illegal task: forming a dreaded force called the Khaki Risala. It was unlawful in the sense that the Meerut garrison commissioner had been tasked with using his resources for only defensive purposes. However, he contrived with Magistrate and Collector Dunlop to constitute this force. It comprised chiefly European troops and some horse-drawn cannons. Whichever village he visited, he would destroy it completely, killing all its inhabitants by setting it on fire, and the survivors were hanged from trees.

Causing unrelenting annihilation in countless villages, he finally headed to Baraut to take on Shahmal. On the way, he also destroyed the village of Basod, killing all its inhabitants; he also set on fire the grain stored there aside for supply to the Delhi army. At Baraut, Shahmal himself launched an attack on the Khaki Risala; he led his farmer army on horseback. While his men sacrificed themselves at the hands of a superiorly equipped force, he himself was unfortunate as his turban was untied to wrap around the horse's feet, bringing him down. At once, he was beheaded; not only this, his head was spiked on a lance for display. This battle is known as the Second Battle of Meerut.

Narpat Singh of Sardhana rose in a similar confrontation. In his village, Akalpura, he drove away the English servants who had come to collect the revenue and went on to attack the tehsil at Sardhana, but he could not succeed. He fortified his village, creating a formidable barrier for the English troops to enter. Finally, the cannons had to be brought, causing great damage to the village. When the Khaki Risala ultimately entered the village, it spared no one. Among hundreds of corpses lay one that of Narpat Singh.

In Mawana tehsil of Meerut, Rao Kadam Singh declared himself the ruler of Mawana and Parikshatgarh. He was the grandson of the last king of Parikshatgarh, Raja Nain Singh, and the brother of Raja Nain Singh. This princely state had been occupied by the English in 1818. He dug out the three cannons, buried in 1803, and mounted them on the fort. He is believed to have an army of 10,000 fighters, who wore white turbans. He came in contact with the revolutionaries from Bareilly and planned an extensive campaign for freedom. There is information about his activities until April 1858, when he was preparing for the invasion of Meerut together with Nawab Mahmood Khan of Bijnor. After the revolutionaries were beaten in Bareilly, Mahmood Khan was captured. There is no information on what happened to Rao Kadam Singh after this.

The village Sikri Khurd, located on the Meerut-Delhi Highway near Modinagar, emerged as a centre of revolutionary activities. A youth army was dispatched to Delhi under the command of Tunda Singh Chandela; however, it had to return to the village following a skirmish with the English troops on the way. After this, they plundered the treasury at Begumabad and fortified the village. When the Khaki Risala attacked, every person who could take up arms joined in the effort, only to sacrifice himself. An intense battle also took place in a large building in the village. The remaining old men and children took refuge in the temple's underground shelter. The English searched them out, and all of them were hanged from the banyan tree located in the temple premises. The number of people thus martyred is believed to be 121. This temple is today known as the Mahamaya Temple. The Goddess's image here is herself a witness to this barbaric event. Following the massacre, the women sacrificed themselves as they jumped into a massive fire that was lit on a farm, today called Satiyon Ka Khet.

If we begin to describe all the revolutionary villages of Meerut, it would be an endless narration. Some of the villages that offered extensive sacrifices include Gagol, Panchli Khurd, Bijrol, Dhaulana, Sardhana, Iktiapur, Akalpura, Nagla, Behsuma, Baghu, Tikri, Singhavali, Baleni and scores of others. The 1857 Uprising has left its mark on the psyche, continuing to shake people. Eyes turn wet when the sacrifices are recalled. Some revolutionary villages, like Basod, have suffered a tragedy they have not yet recovered from.

This extensive Uprising had an extensive aftermath. The English brutally repressed it in one year, and in two years, it was completely subdued. It laid the foundation for the Indian freedom struggle in the years that followed, which ultimately brought the light of freedom in 1947. The prediction by the saints came true that the Company's rule would come to an end one hundred years after the battle of Plassey. After the Uprising, the British government took over India's administration.

Swami Dayanand had expressed apprehensions of the failure of the Uprising even before it had occurred. Later, he described it as *Pallavgrahi*, or a revolution that watered the leaves and not the roots, as he found the Indians not yet united and ready for it. Today we are free, yet the elements of disunity have been sown amongst us in the frivolous names of caste, religion, region and language. Without true unity, the dream of the Vishwaguru Bharat would remain elusive; maybe a still larger Uprising would be needed for that.

Krantigeet or Song of Revolution

Appendix 'A'

Ham hain iske malik, yeh Hindustan hamara, Paak watan hai kaum ka, Jannat se bhi pyara. Yeh hai hamari milkiyat, Hindustan hamara, Iski ruhaniyat se roshan hai jag sara. Kitna Kadeem, kitna naim, sab duniya se nyara, Karti hain jarkhej jise Ganga-Jamna ki dhara. Upar barfila parvat pahredar hamara, Niche sahil par bajta sagar ka nakkara. Iski khanen ugal rahi hain sona heera para, Iski shano-shaukat ka duniya mein jaikara. Aaya Firangi door se aisa mantar mara, Loota donon hathon se pyara watan hamara. Aaj shaheedo ne tum ko E ahle watan pukara, Tod ghulami ki janjeeren, barsao angara. Hindu, Muslim, Sikh hamara bhai pyara-pyara, Yah hai azadi ka jhanda, Ise salaam hamara.	We are her masters, this Hindustan is ours. The sacred nation of the race, lovelier than the paradise. She is our asset, Hindustan is ours. Her spirituality enlightens the whole world. How ancient, how pleasant, unique from the world. The streams of Ganga-Yamuna anoint her. With the snowy mountain guarding us above. And with the ocean drumming down below. Her mines produce gold, diamond and mercury. The world hails her splendour. The European came from afar to cast a spell. He plundered our lovely nation badly. Today our martyrs call upon you O lovely nation To break free of the shackles of slavery and fight furiously. We Hindus, Muslims, Sikhs are all brothers. This is our flag of freedom, and we salute her.

Note: This song was popular among the native sepoys and revolutionaries taking part in the 1857 Uprising. Its words clearly indicate that they had not been fighting for any religion or faith, but for an ideal nation.

List of 85 Sepoys Who Refused to Use the Controversial Cartridges

Appendix 'B'

Havildar Matadin, Naik Sheikh Peer Ali, Naik Ameer Kudrat Ali, Naik Sheikh Husainuddin, Naik Sheikh Noor Muhammad, Sheetal Singh, Jahangir Khan, Meer Mausim Ali, Ali Noor Khan, Meer Hussain Baksh, Mathura Singh, Narayan Singh, Lal Singh, Shyodan Singh, Sheikh Hussain Baksh, Sahib Dad Khan, Bishan Singh, Baldev Singh, Sheikh Nandu, Nawab Khan, Sheikh Ramzan Ali, Ali Mohammad Khan, Makkhan Singh, Durga Singh (I), Nasuralla Beig, Mehrab Khan, Durga Singh (II), Nabi Baksh Khan, Zurkan Singh (I), Zurkan Singh (II), Bhudgu Khan, Abdulla Khan, Ahsan Khan, Zabardast Khan, Murtaza Khan, Baljor Singh, Azimulla Khan (I), Azimulla Khan (II), Kallan Khan, Sheikh Sadulla, Salar Baksh Khan, Sheikh Rahat Ali, Dwarika Singh, Kalka Singh, Raghuvir Singh, Baldev Singh, Darshan Singh, Imdad Hussain, Murad Peer Khan, Moti Singh, Sheikh Fazal Imam, Heera Singh, Sewa Singh, Murad Peer Khan, Sheikh Aram Ali, Kashi Singh, Ashraf Ali Khan, Qadar Dad Khan, Sheikh Rustam, Bhagwan Singh, Meer Imdad Baksh, Shiv Baksh Singh, Laxman Singh, Sheikh Imam Baksh, Usman Khan, Daryab Singh, Maqsood Ali Khan, Sheikh Ghasi Khan, Sheikh Ummed Ali, Abdul Wahab Khan, Ram Sahay Singh, Panah Ali Khan, Lakshman Dube, Ramsharan Singh, Sheikh Khwaja Ali, Shiv Singh, Sheetal Singh, Mohan Singh, Vilayat Ali Khan, Sheikh Muhamma Ejaz, Inder Singh, Fateh Khan, Maiku Khan, Sheikh Qasim Ali, Ram Saran Singh.

Bibliography

English Books:

- By One Who Has Served Under Sir Charles Napier, *The Mutiny of the Bengal Army*, Bosworth and Harrison, London, 1858.
- Tandan, R.K., *Hanged For Their Patriotism*, National Book Trust, India, New Delhi.
- Agarwal, B.R., *Trials of Independence*, National Book Trust, India, New Delhi.
- Iqbal Hussain, *Bakht Khan*, National Book Trust, India, New Delhi.
- Majumdar, R.C., Roychaudhury, H.C. & Dutta, Kalikinkar, *An Advanced History of India*, MacMillan.
- Sharda, Har Bilas, *Life of Dayanand Saraswati*, Ajmer, 1946.
- Kaye, John William, *A History of the Sepoy War in India*, in 4 Vols, Longmans, Green and Co., Bombay, 1896.
- Kaye, J.W. & Malleson, G.B., *Indian Mutiny of 1857-8*, W.H. Allen & Co., London, 1889.
- Paunchkouree Khan, *The Revelations of an Orderly*, E.J. Lazarus & Co., 1866.
- Madhukar Upadhyay, *1857 The Great March Meerut to Delhi*, Ministry of Information and Broadcasting, Government of India, New Delhi.
- Amit Pathak, Dr., *1857 Living History*, U.P. Government Museum, Jhansi.
- Newill, H.R. (comp. & ed.) *Meerut A Gazetteer, District Gazetteers of the United Provinces of Agra and Awadh*, Vol. IV, 1904.
- Srikumar, A.K., *Our Leaders*, Children's Book Trust, New Delhi.
- Keene, Henry George, *Fifty Seven – Some Account of the Administration in Indian Districts During the Revolt of the Bengal Army*, W.H. Allen & Co., London, 1883.
- Rai, Lala Lajpat, *Young India*, National Book Trust, India, New Delhi.

- Sharma, L.P., *History of Modern India*, Konark Pub., Delhi.
- Max Muller, F., *Auld Lang Syne* (*My Indian Friends*), Charles Scribner & Sons, New York, 1899.
- Datta, K.K., Dr., *Biography of Kunwar Singh and Amar Singh*, K.P. Jayaswal Research Institute, Patna, 1957.
- Blavatsky, Helena Petrovna, *From the Caves and Jungles of Hindostan*, The Theosophical Publishing Society, London, 1908 (Reprint).
- Dutta, Dr. K.K., *Unrest Against the British Rule in Bihar 1831-1859*, Secretariat Press Patna, 1917.
- Travelyan, G.O., *The Competition Walah*, MacMillan & Co., 1866.
- Abdul Kalam, Dr. A.P.J., *Ignited Minds.*
- *Nehru and Azad on 1857*, National Book Trust, India, 2008.
- Devsare, Harikrishna, *Nana Saheb Peshwa*, Pub. Division, Govt of India, 2011.
- Devsare, Harikrishna, *Tatya Tope*, Pub. Division, Govt of India, 2011.
- Dalrymple, William, *The Last Mughal*, Penguin Random House, 2006.
- Chandra, Bipan, *History of Modern India*, Orient Blackswan, 2009.
- Ahir, Rajiv, I.P.S., *A Brief History of Modern India*, Spectrum Books (P) Ltd, 2014.
- Sheorey, Indumati, *Tatya Tope*, National Book Trust, India, 1973.

Hindi Books:

- Deepankar, Acharya, *Swadhinata Andolan aur Meerut*, Janmat Pub., Meerut.
- Jain, Rekha, *Swadhinata Sangram*, National Book Trust, India, New Delhi.
- Gupta, Vijay Kumar, *Bharat Ki Mahan Krantikari Mahilaen*, Suruchi Pub., New Delhi.
- Varni, Rajyogi Acharya Bhadrakam (Ed.), *Yogi Ka Atmacharitra*, Aryasamaj Mandir, Delhi.
- Joshi, P.C. (ed.), *Inquilab 1857*, National Book Trust, India, New Delhi.
- Adityamuni Vanprastha, Er., and Vedvrit 'Alok', Dr., (Eds.), *Apna Janmacharitra*, Ganga Pub., Bhopal.

- Adityamuni Vanprastha, Er., *Janmatithi*, Ganga Pub., Bhopal.
- Pandey, Kamaladutt (Ed.), *Hindu Panch Balidaan Ank*, National Book Trust, India, New Delhi.
- Sharda, Dewan Bahadur Harbilas, *Vishwa Guru Swami Dayanand Ka Jeevan Charit Evam Unki Shikshaen*, Sri Ghurmal Prahladkumar Arya Dharmartha Nyas, Hindon City (Rajasthan).
- Adityamuni Vanprastha, Er., *Ajnat Jeevan*, Ganga Pub., Bhopal.
- Singh, B.K., *Swami Dayanand*, National Book Trust, India, New Delhi.
- Nirmohi, Deepchandra, *Kaljayi Sant*, Sarvakalyan Dharmarth Nyas, Panipat.
- Valimbe, V.S., *1857 Ka Sangram*, National Book Trust, India, New Delhi.
- Savarkar, Vinayak Damodar, *1857 Ka Swatantrya Samar*, Prabhat Paperbacks, New Delhi.
- Dayanand Saraswati, *Satyarth Prakash*, Arsha Sahitya Prachar Trust, Delhi.
- Sharma, Nidhi, Dr., *1857*, Bharat Jnan Vijnan Samiti, New Delhi.
- Gautam, Manoj Kumar, Dr., *Bharatiya Swatantrata Andolan Satat Prayas*, Government Freedom Struggle Museum, Meerut.
- Aryamuni Vanaprastha, *Mahrishi Swami Dayanand Ka Meerut Pravas*, Acharya Vishwabandhu Manav Sevarth Nyas, Muzaffarnagar, U.P.
- Adityamuni Vanaprastha, Er., *Dayanand-Divakar*, Ganga Pub., Bhopal.
- Nirmohi, Deepchandra, *Kaljayi Sant*, Sarvakalyan Dharmarth Nyas, Panipat.
- Rizvi, Syed Atahar Abbas, Dr., *Swatantra Dilli*, Uttar Pradesh Hindi Sansthan, Lucknow.
- Gandhi, A.K., *1857 Kranti Va Krantidhara*, National Book Trust, India, New Delhi, 2016.

About the author

A.K. Gandhi is a historian, author and translator. He writes in both Hindi and English and has several books to his credit, published by prestigious publishers including the National Book Trust (*1857 Kranti Va Krantidhara*), Madhya Pradesh Hindi Granth Akademi, Bhopal (*Pratap, Shivaji aur Chhatrasal*), Kitabghar Pub. (*Bharatiya Thal Sena: Badhate Kadam*), Prabhat Pub. (*Subhas—Death That Wasn't, Swami Ramdev*), Fingerprint Pub. (*Dance to Freedom*), Atlantic Pub. (*Mahrishi Dayanand aur 1857 Kranti*), and others. The book *Pratap, Shivaji aur Chhatrasal* busted several myths about the three legendary leaders, impressed by which the Madhya Pradesh Govt rewarded it by including it in the state education syllabus as supplementary study for class XI. His articles, stories and views have appeared in several prestigious newspapers and magazines including the Pustak Sanskriti, the Hindu, Times of India, Reader's Digest, Outlook, Competition Success Review, Amar Ujala, Janwani, Dainik Jagran, and others.

As a translator, he has several published books to his credit, including *Gond*, *Komagata Maru* (both Eng-Hindi, National Book Trust), *The Battle of Rezang La* (Eng-Hindi; Penguin – NBT) and Narendra Modi's *Jyotipunj* (Hindi-Eng, Prabhat Pub.), among others.

An ex-IAF language specialist, A.K. Gandhi has also been the Mentor under the Prime Minister Yuva Mentorship Scheme (for young authors), as part of the Azadi Ka Amrit Mahotsav programme